PUBLIC PRAISE

Celebrating Jesus on the Streets of the World

GRAHAM KENDRICK

Foreword by John Dawson

Creation House
Strang Communications Company
190 North Westmonte Drive
Altamonte Springs, FL 32714
(407) 862-7565

Unless otherwise noted, all Scripture quotations
are from the New American Standard Bible.
Copyright © 1960, 1962, 1963, 1968, 1971, 1972,
1973, 1975, 1977 by the Lockman Foundation.
Used by permission.

Scripture quotations marked KJV are from the
King James Version of the Bible.

Scripture quotations marked NIV are from
the Holy Bible, New International Version.
Copyright © 1973, 1978, 1984, International
Bible Society. Used by permission.

ACKNOWLEDGMENTS

With heartfelt thanks to my wife, Jill, and daughters, Abigail, Amy, Tamsin and Miriam for lending me to this writing project so uncomplainingly. Without their understanding and sacrifice it could not have been written, and much of what the book was written about could not have taken place. A book is rarely the product of one person's effort.

In that respect special thanks is given to Steve Hawthorne for sharpening and expanding my thinking, for creating order out of a chaotic manuscript, for the bulk of chapter 11 and for adding new shades of meaning to the word *tenacity*.

Thanks to Jean and Janice for their dedication to the seemingly endless task of typing, checking and retyping; to Geoff and Jean for sharing the pressure; to Hilary for research and help in kick-starting the early chapters; to Tom and Theresa Pelton for the appendices; to Linda Riesberry for telling her own praise march story; and to all at March for Jesus U.K. for being part of the story.

Thanks to Walter Walker and his editorial staff at Creation House for fulfilling impossible deadlines.

Finally, thanks to all those who have prayed me through, especially the Ichthus Christian Fellowship, whose love for Jesus and obedience to the task of world evangelization has been a fertile seedbed for public praise.

CONTENTS

FOREWORD

Do you need some good news?

This book is a testimony of the sovereign Creator at work in the world today. Something about this story makes me want to weep and shout for joy. Jesus is risen! He rules in the midst of His people.

Our matchless King is being seen, becoming known for who He really is. His church is proclaiming in the streets the overwhelming fact of time and eternity. "God is good, and His mercy endures forever!"

We are not an abandoned generation sliding toward inevitable darkness. God's kingdom strengthens like the rising of a relentless tide.

Who would have predicted that a revelation of the majesty of the Word would flood into the nations at this time? Who would have predicted that the once-shrunken and discouraged church of Britain would lead the way?

In recent years, churches all over Great Britain have been taking to the streets with praise, prayer and proclamation in joyful processions and open-air celebrations. Mostly they have joined together with Christians of churches other than their own, united by a common desire to exalt the name of Jesus where they live. Together they have made an impact on a scale which would not be possible in isolation. From the chill of Christmas shopping centers to the sunshine (and occasional rain) of streets, parks and city squares, hundreds of thousands of people have taken part in local and citywide marches. At the heart of these events have been the songs from the *Make Way* albums, written especially as musical tools for the streets, married to Scripture proclamations, prayers and responsive shouts.

Countless Christians are discovering a new boldness in confessing their love for Christ as they joyfully pour out their praise and proclaim His lordship without shame or apology. They unite in repentance, humility and supplication, calling upon God to revive His church and bring a great spiritual awakening to the nation. In the process they are learning new skills and building new relationships as organizers work with police and local authorities to establish rapport in the community. Also, musicians and worship leaders have discovered how their skills can provide a platform for others to experience God's presence in the open air.

Against this background of Make Way marches, the annual March for Jesus has become firmly established as a national event in the United Kingdom, growing rapidly from 15,000 to 200,000 participants. Local and citywide marches and street events happen throughout the year, but March for Jesus is a unique opportunity to make an impact on a national scale in any country. It is a day to exalt and honor Jesus Christ together before government and people and before all powers of the earth and heaven.

As the ripples from these events go out, the joyful

invasion of the streets in Jesus' name is fast becoming an international phenomenon. The day is upon us when we can participate with Christians all around the world in a twenty-four-hour praise march. Believers will circle the globe with a proliferation of joyful celebrations in honor of Jesus as the earth spins through the time zones, and the sun rises and sets upon people of every tribe and tongue and nation.

I believe that what we are witnessing is a fulfillment of Isaiah's prophecy when he said, "The Sovereign Lord will make righteousness and praise spring up before all nations" (Is. 61:11, NIV).

That which is birthed in God's kingdom is first conceived in praise. Because worship is becoming our priority we are putting off the shackles of unbelief. The river of life is flowing out again. The Lord is near, and His mercy is poured out. The grace of God is revealed for the healing of our nations.

John Dawson
Chairman, March for Jesus U.S.A.
Advisory Council
London, England
April 1992

INTRODUCTION

These things His disciples did not understand
at the first (John 12:16).

The apostle John made this comment concerning
the disciples' failure to grasp the prophetic significance of what is known to us as the triumphal
entry. It was not until much later, after Jesus was glorified,
that a fuller understanding dawned upon them. Those of
us who have been caught up in taking the praises of Jesus
onto the streets feel that we have something in common
with those bemused disciples: we had no idea what we
were getting ourselves into either! Even after living with
it for a number of years now, I still hesitate to claim
anything like a full grasp of its meaning or significance.
We began with more intuition than understanding, with
more enthusiasm than skill, and tried like Paul to obey
the "heavenly vision," though it often seemed foolish,
risky and occasionally unwelcome (Acts 26:19).

We did not see the end from the beginning and still
don't, but as we took each step of obedience, it became a
little clearer where to place the next footstep. We never

had a master plan of our design or an assumption that the concept would have any future beyond that next step we had agreed on in faith. But we had to give a title to the growing movement of internationally coordinated public praise marches, and it was March for Jesus.

I have the habit of saying that we don't run March for Jesus; we run after it. Time after time when we make our next-step plan, events overtake us, the vision is surpassed, and we find ourselves breathless in pursuit of the thing. At its basic level it is no more than a concept and not entirely a new one at that. But somehow it has taken on a life of its own and reproduces itself. We discovered some time ago that it was bigger than those of us who have carried the torch for it in the United Kingdom. Consequently we have tried to recognize the danger of attempting to control it. Rather, as we run after it and try to give it away, we are jealous only over its purity lest it mutate into something other than what it was meant to be.

As a concept its safeguard is that it has no life unless it is adopted and owned by the rank and file of the churches and their leaders. It has no power unless the Holy Spirit breathes into the people as they do it. As an overflow of admiration for Jesus, it cannot happen unless people's hearts are brimming.

The seedbed which facilitated the rapid growth of March for Jesus in England was friendship. The embryonic vision came through many individuals who were friends. It was confirmed and strengthened as they prayed and dreamed dreams together. The first major march, called the City march (through the historic section of old London), happened because of three friends: Roger Forster, pastor of Ichthus Christian Fellowship; Gerald Coates, Pioneer Ministries; and C. Lynn Green, European director for Youth With A Mission. They obeyed the vision by putting the combined resources of their church networks and organizations behind it. Personal interests were sacrificed for the sake of going forward together. I continue to delight in the way God joins such diverse characters and makes serving Him together so enjoyable.

Rather than running on the tracks of big-money promotional techniques, it flows through networks of friendship and trust among ordinary church leaders. Though it occasionally draws some media attention, it is promoted more through the grapevine than the headline.

Though my name is on this book and associated with many of the songs used on the streets, this was not my idea. Many marches have occurred before these were started. Many people were involved in its inception in our little corner of the world, and many more are involved now. Similar stories could be told from other parts of the world by people whose only connection with us is the Holy Spirit. I dearly hope that this has been one of God's ideas dropped into not a few but countless imaginations, a divine initiative to glorify the magnificent Son of God and to lavish affection upon the One who lavished everything upon us.

ONE

THE CHURCH
ON DISPLAY

We stood on the makeshift platform amazed at the sight of fifty-five thousand singing, smiling Christians as they began a March for Jesus. For an hour we had watched as a seemingly endless stream of banner-carrying believers approached the assembly area across two of London's famous bridges. They crammed the whole highway in both directions in a montage of color and activity. We had listened to the sound of impromptu singing and the squawks and squeals of scores of mobile worship bands making final adjustments to their ensembles or public address systems.

The scene was the March for Jesus to the Heart of the Nation (1988), and the atmosphere was extraordinary. Smiles were contagious and appeared to have become permanent. The sun was shining, and even the police escorts were beginning to relax and enjoy the occasion.

A forest of banners rose like a living thing as the great procession slowly got underway. Children rode in strollers or on shoulders. People of every age, color and class linked arms. The disabled moved in wheelchairs. Here and there the more agile broke into impromptu ring dances. Musicians tried to walk and play at once. Stewards marshalled the crowds. Supervisors spoke urgently into walkie-talkies.

In a cacophony of sound, each section in unison followed the printed program of songs, prayers, Scripture verses and shouts. The voices of singers and prayer leaders crackled through their sound systems. Praise and prayer echoed around streets more used to the babble of tourists or the angry shouts of political demonstrations.

Roger Forster, who led one of the groups of churches sponsoring the march, wept at the sight. Having ministered for more than thirty years in a climate of church decline and pessimism, he had never expected to live long enough to see this many believers gathered in one place with such a sense of hope and purpose.

Why did the marchers come, many from far-flung corners of the nation? "We're marching for Jesus." "We're here to proclaim to the nation that Jesus is Lord." "We want to stand up and be counted for Jesus." "We're praying for revival." "We love Jesus." The same sentiments came irrespective of denomination and church tradition; distinctions had melted away, and hearts had melted together as everyone gave glory to God at the heart of the nation.

Soon we passed the Ministry of Defense, the government buildings of Whitehall, the prime minister's residence, the houses of Parliament and the headquarters of multinational companies. An hour later we reached Hyde Park, singing hoarsely, "Shine, Jesus, shine — fill this land with the Father's glory."

There, exhausted but exhilarated, the marchers settled into a spontaneous mass picnic with outbreaks of prayer, singing or general enjoyment continuing into the early evening. The media had sent TV crews to find out why we were there; a report was broadcast that evening on the national news watched by twelve million viewers.

If anybody had come wondering why we were marching for Jesus, they were more likely to end the day asking, Why had we waited so long? For many believers coming from small churches and struggling for a sense of significance in an increasingly secular society, the experience was intoxicating. It was a turning point for them to discover they are actually part of a large movement as they shared a program, a sense of God's presence and a passion for revival with believers from other towns and other traditions (even ones they might disagree with). They felt a new sense of visibility as the police closed street after street to traffic just for them, and they saw themselves on national TV later that evening. It all added up to a powerful message: There is one Lord, one faith. There is one church, and it is on the move with one purpose in mind, to proclaim Jesus King of the nation and to see His kingdom come and His will be done on earth as it is in heaven!

The Invisible Church

The church has rarely been on display in such festive light. To very many people the church hardly exists because they never see it. Rare visits for christenings, weddings and funerals plus the images conveyed by television programs may only serve to create an unhelpful caricature.

People assume that what goes on inside a church building has very little to do with them. Even where research shows that a large majority of a population believes in God, their absence on Sunday indicates they don't think that what happens in church could help them find Him. They are probably happier to look in other directions to find out what or who this God might be.

The assumption needs to be challenged that the church should get on quietly with the business of religion and let the rest of the world get on with its business undisturbed. It has been fascinating to read reports of how the attitudes of local authorities have been changed by marches taking place. For example, skeptical police authorities expect only a few hundred people even though the organizers plan for thousands. By the end of the day they will have witnessed not only a vast gathering of believers but an atmosphere of joy. Plus they will see a group within society that can be trusted to fill the streets with goodwill and even leave the city cleaner than when they came.

A leading clergyman in one city complained that praise marches disrupted the smooth running of the city by slowing down traffic and making people late for their appointments. This seemed to be a rather shortsighted view. You can't have a mass demonstration of worship on the streets without having to shut off a few roads and disrupt the normal process of things for an hour or so. In one sense I think the church exists to disrupt the normal running of things in order to draw attention to Jesus. Imagine the chaos that Jesus caused throughout His ministry as crowds gathered. People left their workplaces and turned out in the thousands to hear Him preach. There was considerable disruption when the apostle Paul visited Ephesus and numerous other places.

The church has been apologetic about its presence for far too long. It has been too scared to upset the status quo. It is time we upset the status quo in the most positive way possible and distract people from normal business on a mass scale to get them thinking and talking about Jesus.

For too long we have abdicated responsibility for the

public, visible declaration of our faith. We have effectively abandoned the streets to political marches, activists, cults, charity collectors, carnivals and, in many cases, to seedy street life and an atmosphere of violence. Of course political activity and carnivals can be entirely legitimate, but surely it is time to invade the streets once again in the name of Christ. What right do we Christians have to complain about the state of our streets if we are never there? How can we complain when we have consistently abandoned them to the powers of darkness for decades?

The church needs visibility to be a body of opinion and a group of significance in the life of the nation. Surely one of the best ways to become visible is in the activity to which God has called us and which is our eternal destiny — worship.

In the act of worship the life of Christ within us and our thankfulness to Him for what He has done for us overflow. In this overflow, His life becomes visible and the glory of God shines.

TWO

WHY MARCH?

Such a unified and festive display of Christians raises the obvious question of why we are marching at all. The singular intent of March for Jesus is to exalt Jesus and to see His kingdom come and His will be done on earth. What now seems so obvious a rationale for taking the church to the streets has not always been so clear. The whole process has been and continues to be a voyage of discovery. It has mostly been in retrospect that we have understood a little more of why we should do it and what purpose it serves.

At the beginning we were bemused and hesitant in the same way the two disciples may have been when Jesus sent them for the colt and its mother. "And the disciples went and did just as Jesus had directed them, and brought the donkey and the colt" (Matt. 21:6-7). They weren't at all sure of why Jesus wanted a donkey. In fact, Jesus anticipated questions into their doings. "If anyone says to you, 'Why are you doing this?' you say, 'The Lord has need of it' " (Mark 11:3).

In the same way, we have moved ahead in the unfolding of the March for Jesus with a simple certainty of obedience. To the logical thinker this might seem a strange way to go about something on such a scale; yet, if we are honest, most of us go about our daily lives in more intuitive ways than we might care to admit. Marching was like having a single piece of a jigsaw puzzle but no idea what the whole picture might look like. Similarly our personal spiritual pilgrimage rarely begins with a master plan. Rarely do we see ahead of time the full significance of what is begun when we sow a mustard seed of faith.

So the starting point for March for Jesus was not understanding but obedience. A few of us shared a conviction that God wanted praise on the streets. An understanding grew as we proceeded, despite all the mistakes we made. I knew God was requiring me to write praise march songs, but the call only made sense to me after I began to do it.

In the end, anybody who organizes a March for Jesus must be able to say with confidence that God told him or her to do it. Roger Forster, part of the international board of directors for the March for Jesus, has written: "Why does God work like this? Because revelation must be involved with, if not preceded by, obedience. It is as we obey God that we engage with and enter into the truth of His Word. We do not adequately understand the Scriptures until we are prepared to do them (John 7:17). It is the Holy Spirit who leads us into all truth (John 16:13), and the theology of marching will emerge as we engage in it and listen to what the Spirit is saying."

As we have obeyed God over the past few years, something of an understanding has unfolded. One of the purposes of this book is to clarify this in more detail. I will begin with an overview of what I believe lies at the heart of public praise, especially the praise march.

One Purpose: Passionate Love

Inspired by a line from an old hymn, I included this lyric in a Christmas street song: "But the many gifts He gives are all poured out from one; come receive the greatest Gift, the gift of God's own Son." Similarly, many precious gifts pour out through public praise events, but they are all poured out from one source. Many spiritual dynamics can be identified, but their origin is in one supreme dynamic. Many legitimate motives could be accumulated to present a persuasive argument for taking the walls off the church. But I believe one paramount purpose, one pure motive, holds all the rest together. That motive is a passionate love for Jesus Christ.

How easily we become distracted from God's number one requirement, to love Him with all our hearts, minds, strength and wills. How difficult it is for us in a goal-oriented society to justify to ourselves and to one another giving great tracts of time and expensive resources solely to the expression of our love for the Creator who became our Savior. Yet we know that love for and love from God are the very reason for our existence and the place where each of us began when we first believed.

In case this sounds lofty and super-spiritual against the background of a world brimming with practical needs, I must emphasize that love relationships with God manifest themselves in intensely practical ways. Jesus made it clear that love for Him was inseparable from action, most notably in the way it is tested by how we treat those made in His image, our neighbors. Those who love Him will keep His commandments. Those who obey His command to love their enemies will go the extra humiliating mile carrying their enemies' baggage.

So I am not talking about taking a mere feeling or a state of euphoria onto the streets. In actual fact it is a relationship we take there. This is an awe-inspiring concept. We are not just singing about God; this is not just a novel way of disseminating information about Him. It is a celebration of His presence, not a celebration in the absence of the honored guest, like a birthday party where the one whose party it is has failed to arrive. We focus on the One we love, who is lifted high upon our praises, receiving gifts of worship, praise, thanksgiving and honor, hearing our prayers. He is actually there, where considerably more than two or three are gathered in His name, and we lavish upon Him the love of our hearts before people and angels. We praise Him because of who He is. We thank Him for what He has done. We applaud Him for what He is going to do. We worship Him because He is supremely worthy to receive all worship from everything that has breath.

But I hear someone ask, What does all this achieve? My answer is simple: the Lord receives worship. Not only that, but mankind and angels watch Him receive worship. Is that not an achievement of great significance in the streets of a town or city where He is not normally honored and where the capacity for worship is squandered on worthless things? Is there any higher purpose than this — to bring pleasure to the God who created us and gave the Son He loved as a ransom for us?

For us to arrive home from the streets assured that God has received worship has inestimable value. Yet when the spiritual and physical energies of multitudes of believers are lavished upon Him to glorify Him, many secondary dynamics come into play with a potentially powerful effect. Certainly other products are generated from the exercise, but to seek them is not the highest motive.

Rather we seek the glory of the One who is the object of the event. Equally, we must not be diverted by the excitement of the process by which He is being glorified, the march itself, though we should enjoy it thoroughly. Once we have satisfied ourselves that the Lord has received glory and honor, we can assess what was produced and how much we enjoyed the process.

What a March Is Not

The church is bulging with programs and projects, campaigns and ministries, which, provided they are divinely initiated, are a great thing. But anybody responsible for the success of one of these programs may decide a large gathering of festive Christians is a promotional opportunity. This may be entirely appropriate in the right circumstances, but it may also be the "kiss of death." A multiplicity of agendas is always waiting in the wings for a chance to take center stage, all with apparently legitimate claims for the support of the people. This is particularly true when a movement rises from the grass-roots level and takes on a life and momentum of its own, the way praise marching has gathered great crowds.

Hence, equally important to understanding what a public praise event is, is understanding what it is not.

1. Marches are not protests. The purpose of public praise marches is to affirm and declare our love for Jesus and the truth about Him even though protest is often a valid form of expression for Christians simply because the kingdom we belong to conflicts with the world's kingdom. There is a time for protest, but this is not it.

2. Marches are not built around issues but around a Person. Issues are implicitly there, because Jesus takes issue with the world and convicts it of sin, righteousness and judgment. But those issues are not the main attraction

of a praise march — He is. When He comes to a city, He will convict and convince.

3. Marches are not critical or confrontational. We do not take to the streets to criticize unbelievers but to share the love of Jesus with them, the same love with which He loved us when "we were yet sinners" (Rom. 5:8). We are not there to wrestle with flesh-and-blood enemies but to announce liberty to captives.

4. Marches are not a publicity stunt. God will receive our praises and hear our prayers whether or not we receive TV or newspaper coverage. God can bring about His purposes through us with or without the media. However, our desire to exalt Jesus can include respectfully informing media agencies of the nature and purpose of the event.

5. Marches are not an evangelistic campaign. They may create a climate for evangelism, precipitate salvation for some and be followed with evangelistic initiatives. But in themselves they are God-ward activities which people are invited to witness, and if they are willing, they may be drawn to Christ.

6. Marches are not presented as a method of spiritual warfare. Though we are aware that they have tremendous potential to displace evil spiritual powers, our eyes are upon the captain of heaven's armies, not His enemies. As we put our feet down in His name, we may find that whether consciously or not we have trodden upon "serpents and scorpions." This happens beneath our feet while our eyes are occupied with the glories of Jesus.

7. Marches are not a ritual. They are not merely a new item to round out the Christian calendar, though certain dates may add special significance to a march. They are not routine, but prophetic, not arbitrarily planned, but move best when God is moving in this particular way. Success is not guaranteed; a march only works when God

comes. Marches are a time for festivity but much more than a mass picnic.

8. Marches are not triumphalism, a way to promote one doctrine as superior to all others. Though we celebrate, we may also find ourselves weeping, repenting or publicly humbling ourselves. We are celebrating the triumph of Christ, so we should remember that He triumphed through humility, servanthood and suffering. At the other extreme, we do not encourage any tendency toward a soulish indulgence of "evangelical" guilt.

9. Marches are not personality-centered. Of course people need to be led, and leaders need to be seen. But this is not the time to parade personalities, rather to praise a Person. Because of my association with public praise marches, I am sometimes invited as a special guest. Though grateful and willing to serve where I can, I find it difficult to know what to do there because a march is essentially a "people" event. I sometimes get asked to march at the front with local leaders. But as far as the marchers are concerned, they can see only the backs of the heads of the row in front of them. The British press has been frequently bewildered at the apparent absence of leaders. In this we delight because there is less to draw the attention away from Jesus.

THREE

Grass-Roots Beginnings

S oho in London's West End is famous for its night life. It is bordered by theaters, cinemas and restaurants, and it has a seedier underside of strip clubs, prostitution and drugs. On a Saturday evening these narrow streets channel an endless stream of theatergoers, fun seekers and tourists from all over the world. But this Saturday in the fall of 1985 was different. In the distance a sound uncharacteristic of the area grew until suddenly a crowd of people burst into view. The sound of praise filled the air, turning heads and interrupting the street entertainers. It was something that Soho had never seen before: a praise march.

It was not only new to the streets of Soho; it was new to many of its participants, including me. As part of the Ichthus Christian Fellowship and together with Youth With A Mission, I had joined a crowd of believers to participate in the early stages of establishing a permanent ministry base in Soho. However, the main purpose of the march was not evangelism. It was a spiritual exercise: an act of prayer, an act of proclamation that the kingdom of God was coming. It would be a prophetic act — a symbol of the fact that the church was determined to establish itself in that area.

Not knowing quite what to expect, we piled into a few minibuses, drove up and gathered in a small back-street premises run by YWAM (pronounced y-wam). We had only expected a small group of people, but about three hundred of us crammed into the tiny rooms and up the stairs. After some prayer we divided into groups of about thirty. This was because permission had not been obtained from the police in time for us actually to march the streets en masse, so we had to use the sidewalks.

It was a very improvised, spontaneous kind of affair. As different groups set off in different directions, we began to sing our way through the streets. No one even had a song list. Anybody with enough initiative had to choose a few songs and decide what to do. We had an unusual assortment of instruments: a violin, a guitar or two, a flute and, the most useful of all, a large bass drum. It could be heard over the traffic and ticket pushers of Leicester Square. Its insistent rhythm somehow glued the songs together and gave some form to our ragtag army.

I felt very embarrassed as we set out, so I smiled a lot! I well remember the curious gazes of the onlookers and a certain amount of snickering. Feeling somewhat foolish, I wondered if this really would do any good. Yet later that evening as I went home, I knew that an idea which had been nagging at me for many months had been confirmed. Even then I had no idea of the consequences that would follow this unusual evening and the project I would begin in the following days.

One encounter left an imprint that I continued to ponder. As we rounded one corner with our motley group of praise marchers, we came across a group of about half a dozen Hare Krishna followers with saffron robes and shaved heads, banging their tambourines. I can remember the somewhat shocked and horrified expressions on their faces as they saw us come around the corner singing and playing noisily. I think we felt a certain degree of satisfaction that we were actually outnumbering them and beating them at their own game.

The sight of the Hare Krishnas caused me to think again about the significance of what they were doing. Why did they go through the streets chanting their mantras and singing and dancing and playing their tambourines? Why have they been doing it all over the world? Was there a spiritual dynamic to it, and if so what was it?

It is interesting to record that some ten days afterward, the local council and the police moved in and closed down scores of the worst of the strip clubs and illegal vice activities. It is impossible to prove a direct cause-and-effect connection, but we took it as an encouragement.

The march was one of several which Ichthus undertook around that time and just one feature of a whole spectrum of prayer, evangelism and social action activities. As a result of all this, a new congregation began. Now, six years later, a congregation is meeting each Sunday morning for worship in the area. Three hostels for the homeless have been opened; a full-time worker living in the heart of Soho has built up a strong Christian work among prostitutes; Bibles have been placed in every theater dressing room in the West End and Bible studies held in several theater locations.

But one story which was of special encouragement to me came several years later when I happened to ask a young man named Greg how he became a Christian. This is what he told me:

I was standing outside the Odeon Cinema in Leicester Square one day with my girlfriend and a group of other friends when a group of these happy-clappy people came past who I immediately realized were Christians. My friends and particularly my girlfriend mocked them, but I remember thinking at the time, I really should be with them.

It had been three years previously that I had met some Christians and been prayed with. About three weeks afterward (to use the jargon) I backslid. Seeing those praise marchers made a major impact which culminated at the end of that year in recommitting myself to God. It was one of those significant points at which God broke into my life and was a major part in the process of Him leading me back to Himself.

Experimenting With Music

We had no clear way of anticipating any kind of fruit resulting from the Soho march at the time. But I do remember coming home that night with a sense of exhilaration in my spirit along with a sore throat and several broken guitar strings. Despite our improvised disorder and my embarrassment, I believed that we had been doing something significant. It was something that was hard to measure — in fact, impossible to evaluate at the time — but in my own heart I felt that it had been important.

Along with this sense of significance, I brought back another conclusion. I felt that we could have actually done it a whole lot better! With the right kind of songs and a more conscious strategy in terms of the content and form, I was convinced that we could be far more effective than we were.

We had struggled throughout the Soho march to think of enough appropriate songs for that situation. The natural thing seemed to be to sing lively praise songs, but I remember on a couple of occasions finding myself halfway through one and thinking, Why on earth are we singing this out here? Words which were perfectly useful and understandable in the context of believers within a church suddenly sounded like nonsense on the streets. I realized how much better we could do if songs were chosen for their relevance outside the church walls or, better yet, if songs were written especially for marches.

I was also aware of the unsuitability of some of the instruments. Unamplified as they were, the violin and the acoustic guitars seemed to disappear into thin air. Attempts to extract more volume out of the instruments often ended in broken strings. I also noticed how easily the group could dissipate if we didn't know what we were supposed to be doing. The momentum would quickly fade as a song ended, and the musicians fumbled around trying to think what to do next.

I set out to make and record a whole sequence of music, Scripture verses and shouts that would be easy to use and simple to learn. I borrowed a few ideas from what I had seen of secular street demonstrations, trying to understand some of the dynamics of a crowd of people spread out down a street. I wanted to create something that could, without endless practices and rehearsals, unite a whole crowd in praise, prayer and proclamation.

This first recording was entitled *Make Way* with a subtitle *A Carnival of Praise*. "Make way" is a colloquial expression in Britain, used, for example, if a security man is trying to clear a way through a crowd for a dignitary. He might well shout, "Make way!" to try to clear a path for the important person to come. I turned this expression into a corporate shout, "Make way for the King of kings," which I felt summed up the essence of what we were doing. We were announcing not ourselves so much as we were that the kingdom of Jesus was coming and that people should prepare and open a pathway for Him into their neighborhood and into their lives.

I chose the word *carnival* to try to express the sense of joy and celebration that I believed should attend the church on the streets. Perhaps this was partly a reaction against some of the expressions of the church I have seen on the streets in the past. Whether it be the sandwich-board man proclaiming, "Prepare to meet thy doom"; hell, fire and damnation preaching; or dreary and embarrassed people huddled together, the message had often been negative. I wanted it to be positive.

Ichthus has always demonstrated that the gospel is good news to the poor. People have enough bad news already, particularly in the urban environment. We needed to proclaim the goodness of God, recognizing that the Scriptures say that it is the goodness of God which leads us to repentance. We wanted to create joyful processions of good news as Jesus did when He travelled with His disciples through the villages and towns of Judea. The ordinary, the common people turned out, brought their sick people and listened intently to this man who had something to say to them. It was a great event; it was positive; it was joyful.

We wanted to communicate to the ordinary people that there was a place of joy, that there was hope, that there was good news for them. We believed that the church worldwide had inherited the mantle which was upon Jesus when in the synagogue of Nazareth He quoted from Isaiah 61:1: "The Spirit of the Sovereign Lord is on me, because the Lord has anointed me to preach good news to the poor" (NIV). We wanted to be good news in our neighborhood. We wanted people to catch the spirit of joy of celebration which was normal inside our buildings but which few of those outside had ever been exposed to.

Our people dressed colorfully and made simple, bright, imaginative banners to wave. We wanted to create a whole event that by its very nature made a statement about the church. Some were even bold enough to dress up in clown costumes and carry balloons. As this whole genre developed, we gave balloons to children on the streets and threw out candies as little tokens of the fact that we brought joy and good news.

The first live use of the album came just a few weeks after it was recorded. It was a march through the streets of Notting Hill, a very cosmopolitan mixed-race area of London, which is famous for its annual carnival parade. From there about three hundred of us got onto the underground train and regathered at Trafalgar Square. Against the background of a more familiar kind of demonstration, a sit-in outside the South African embassy, we marched around the square several times.

By this time I was totally exhausted from having led the songs through a portable public address system, but I felt that, if we kept on doing this, something would break in the heavenly realms. I sensed that we were confronting spiritual powers and threatening the kingdom of darkness.

This first *Make Way* album was released at Easter 1986. We accompanied it with a small booklet giving some practical instructions on how to take praise onto the streets. From our limited experience, we tackled some of the difficulties of welding together a crowd of people strung out along the street, the technicalities of making the music work and the basic organizational necessities. As time went on we were to discover there was much more to learn. When this album was produced, I knew of no other such initiatives outside the Ichthus Christian Fellowship. As far as I knew there was no demand for it; it was just something I felt I should do, a vision which God had put in my heart and which I needed to obey. It wasn't even a dramatic vision. There were no dreams in the night, no startling revelations or angelic visitations. It was just something that had grown little by little in my mind and heart over a period of time. I had an increasing conviction that it needed to be done and a sense that as a songwriter I could make a contribution. It was not even something that I entirely understood.

When the whole vision was taken up with tremendous enthusiasm, I was genuinely surprised. Churches were writing to say they were learning the songs, using the contents of the instruction book and actually taking it onto the streets all around the country. What delighted me even more were the reports of churches from different denominations and traditions joining together to do this thing. Even more conservative ones were joining in. There seemed to be a mood swing in the churches, a sense that the time was right.

One Christian leader said that the churches in our nation had been very much like an underground stream. Many good things had been occurring, but they were hidden. Now was the time for that river to flow out into the open.

Some ordinary church members at a conference also explained that they too wanted to take praise onto the streets, but they had no real starting point until they had come across the *Make Way* album. It fitted in exactly with what they felt the Holy Spirit was telling them to do.

The whole vision was being birthed right from the grass roots. The Make Way marches have been simple, accessible to ordinary believers and open for participation on many levels. Those who can design or sew found endless creative possibilities through making banners. Those with a gift of dance could choreograph new steps and movements for the marchers. The children could carry flags and banners and hold balloons and sing along. The musicians and worship leaders could lead from the back of a truck or walk along the road, depending on the scale of the event. Even where the musical ability was lacking, people simply played the cassette recording and sang with it. That seemed to work well.

Make Way marches proliferated across the country that first year. We had no way of counting how many were taking place, but we had evidence of scores if not hundreds. Often believers were going out for the first time to let their towns or villages know that Christianity was alive and well and on the move. They were mostly small groups — a few hundred people at the most — but some church leaders were planning something bigger.

FOUR

RUNNING AFTER IT

The March for Jesus has emerged from multiple streams. As hearts and visions merge together, we are surprised to find how the movement grows with a life of its own. The structures which serve March for Jesus have come about to serve and not to control. As I have said before, we have a distinct feeling that we do not so much run the March for Jesus as we run after it. This sense of serving and pursuing a vision has grown from the earliest marches.

The City March

The venue for the first big London march in 1987 began as an accident. One of our Ichthus members who worked at the Smithfield meat market asked his bosses if they would give us the huge market building for the weekend. Surprisingly they agreed, and a team met to discuss ideas for its use. They planned to call the event the Festival of the Lamb. The individual shops would be sublet to Christian outlets, children's activities and so on.

But John Pressdee, one of our most down-to-earth but often more visionary Ichthus leaders, felt uneasy about it. "As we prayed I had an intense vision of thousands of people walking around the city of London," John said. "It felt like a heavy responsibility on my shoulders, but the Lord brought me to Joshua 6 and the picture of the Lord as the commander of the heavenly army alongside Joshua. I could almost see walls and strongholds falling."

John took the idea to Roger Forster. Roger in turn shared it with two friends, Lynn Green (YWAM) and Gerald Coates (Pioneer Ministries). They soon realized a march in London was not just one wild idea but several streams flowing together.

YWAM, they discovered, had already researched the historical roots of the city of London and the way it had grown up as a financial power base through the centuries. The YWAMers had already organized a small prayer walk around the city with groups pausing outside many of the major institutions to pray. (A prayer walk lets an intercessor have the target of the prayers in his or her sight. Prayer walking accompanied much of the growth of praise marches. More information will be available in a forthcoming book on the topic by Creation House.)

I had joined them as they assembled for worship on the steps of the corn exchange above whose grand, pillared portico were carved those very words I had already put into song, "The earth is the Lord's and everything in it." The Victorians who built it at least paid lip service to the words, but among the yuppies and money dealers of Thatcherite Britain, God's sovereignty was certainly not a fashionable concept.

A march was called, and I was drawn into the planning as it was decided to incorporate the praise march music from the *Make Way* album that I had written and recorded in the previous year. We suspected that we were onto something big. Through the networks of those who were organizing it, the word was put out. Five thousand or so people were expected to gather at Smithfield market one Saturday in early spring to march through the city.

On Saturdays, the "City" — that historic square mile where the wider city of London had its origins — was not well-populated. Offices emptied on weekends, and there were few shopping streets or residential areas where people gathered. Clearly, if we wanted the praise marching to be visible, this was not the right time or place. But so sure were we of God's prompting that this did not seem to matter. For this march, at least, it was primarily a spiritual exercise.

A route was chosen and negotiated with the police, and a program was prepared and printed, drawing on the historic and contemporary significance of some of the landmarks of the city. As we followed our route we could pray intelligently into the very roots of London life.

We were to pass St. Paul's Cathedral, not only a center of worship and of the institutional church, but a symbol of Londoners' tenacity to survive the blitz of World War II. Further along were the stock exchange; the corn exchange, where the financial futures market operates; and the Old Bailey, where the statue of blindfolded Justice with her scales presides over the highest of the nation's criminal law courts. We were to march along some of the ancient walls and gates of a city that dated back before Christ and had absorbed Anglo-Saxon superstition, Roman philosophy and Renaissance learning along with Christian tradition and blatant materialism.

We would also pass by a memorial to John Wesley, who led one of the greatest national revivals in British history. The brass plaque quotes those pages from his journal where he speaks of being "strangely warmed" by the gospel — how we wanted that same warmth of the Holy Spirit's presence to spread through our city again.

We certainly had no natural warmth that day! It felt like the coldest May day on record. From the start the elemental heavens opened, and torrential rain poured upon us. But the cold and wet did not seem to deter anyone. We were stunned to find that, according to the police, our five thousand estimate had swollen to fifteen thousand. The streets around Smithfield became a sea of umbrellas. Despite the incessant rain the strong spirit of prayer and praise in the crowd indicated a remarkable and significant event.

Eventually the crowd moved. Group by group, musicians from different churches led, singing songs and praying as they went. Clutching their soggy programs, they used them as a guide for praying. For example, when the program noted that the march was passing by the Bank of England extension, the marchers were urged to "pray for the Bank of England, for it to maintain justice and righteousness in all its affairs and for it to act against greed and unrighteousness through its supervisory role."

When the route passed Holborn, London's sales center for precious stones, metal and jewelry, the marchers were to "claim the wealth of the nations for the Lord. Declare your trust in Him rather than all that is precious on earth. Declare that God is on the throne and not mammon (the false god of materialism). Remember, " 'The silver is Mine, and the gold is Mine,' declares the Lord of hosts" (Hag. 2:8).

We felt we should pray particularly concerning issues of righteousness and justice in the financial dealings of the city. We did not want to make an issue of any particular injustice, but research on the spiritual history of the city made it clear that it had been built upon greed and unrighteous trade. We prayed with that in mind, asking that God would deal with greed in the city.

That particular year was quite a boom time. The de-regulation of 1986 had meant that every bank and invest-ment house in the world had wanted to set up in the square mile. Those were heady days on London's money mar-kets, with fortunes waiting to be made. Millions were changing hands at the press of a computer button. The city wine bars were crowded with twenty-five-year-olds taking home £250,000 a year (equal to about $500,000), and their Porsches were parked outside. The boomers were arrogant and self-confident with an accompanying disregard for justice and righteousness.

We had prayed more from historical and spiritual in-sight than from inside knowledge of the financial world, but having prayed along these lines, we were fascinated to read the newspapers in the following months, espe-cially on Black Monday in October 1987 when the global stock market collapsed. Business slumped to record lows. In the following months many new and even well-established companies went bankrupt. An estimated twelve thousand whiz kids lost their jobs. The party was over.

Alongside this, insider dealing was exposed. Some-thing called the Guinness affair broke and began its long journey through the courts, exposing dishonest trading by seemingly respectable establishment figures.

Had our prayers contributed to these events which changed the course of the nation? It is impossible to prove a cause-and-effect connection, and these questions can only truly be answered in eternity. But we took note that the city had been shaken around the very issues of greed and unrighteous trade. Whatever else had combined to cause it, the mercy of God was checking the runaway materialism which was claiming the soul of the nation at that time.

The Movement Grows

The March for Jesus seems to surge ahead with a life of its own. Every fresh initiative lifts off from the last. I suppose we can trace three discernible innovations, each of them seeming natural and almost necessary. The idea of a city march gave rise to the idea of participants coming from all points of the country; and from there it wasn't hard to look forward to scores of marches taking place simultaneously. At that point it was difficult not to envision simultaneous marches taking place in many countries. Even though there never has been a master plan to get the world marching, God has inspired an unfolding vision.

The march in May 1987 through the historical district of London further popularized the growing vision of taking the church onto the streets. Many who were initiated by the City march took the vision home and laid plans for similar events in their neighborhoods and cities, more or less coinciding with the availability of a new praise march music album *Shine, Jesus, Shine*, which was released two years after the original album.

Though the City march had been conceived as a one-time event, the proliferation of local marches was adding to a growing momentum toward another capital city march. We agreed that God was leading us to this. March for Jesus to the Heart of the Nation, set for May 21, 1988, was focused on Westminster, the government district of London. Response was strong. Amid all the excitement, the idea of simultaneous marching throughout the nation emerged.

When everyone had assembled for the march on the Embankment along the Thames River, there were fifty-five thousand people, more than double what had been expected.

Many Cities, One March

The momentum of the movement increased yet again. A day when simultaneous marches would take place in several cities actually became feasible. The title March for Jesus Across the Nation was coined. Twelve major regional marches were proposed for September 16, 1989. These twelve eventually became forty-five. With this came the necessary serving structure of a local organizing committee for each march. March for Jesus Across the Nation coincided with a pioneer long-distance prayer walk, the Torch March. The walk covered the ground from John O'Groats to Lands End, the extreme northern and southern points of Britain. In just three weeks, three teams covered hundreds of miles praying with their words and actions for national revival.

March for Jesus Across the Nation was significant for a number of reasons. As many as 200,000 believers were together with one heart to pray for their land. Underground cable communication lines connected all the marches, so that we were certainly praying "in one accord" and, in a sense, all praying "in one place" (see Acts 2:1, KJV).

Throughout Britain there was a strong pressure from the grass roots to march locally. Thus the idea of March for Jesus Where You Live in 1990 was born. Simultaneous marching took on yet another form. It was designed as a day when hundreds of neighborhood marches would take place at the same time. An estimated 200,000 people marched in 603 separate local marches ranging in size from 10,000 in Belfast to fewer than 20 in some villages.

Following this event, George Carey, then archbishop-designate, commented, "The church has a message to proclaim and should not be embarrassed or frightened to take it into the marketplace or the streets of our communities. Such events are also signs of our unity together because every denomination is involved in this form of witness."

The next year, the same pattern of locally based praise marches drew upwards of 250,000 people in about 750 localities with each march taking on a specially designed evangelism project.

Nations Marching Together

Marches had already emerged in other countries. But with 1992 approaching and its significance for Europe, the vision came forth that churches across Europe should identify together beyond national boundaries and pray for the re-evangelization of Europe. European church leaders were invited to Britain to observe the marches in September 1989 as a first step toward a continent-wide event for 1992.

Sixty European leaders met in Holland to ask the question, Should we do this together? The unanimous response was positive. Out of this came plans for Europe Together, to take place on May 23, 1992. As of this writing, forty-eight marches are planned in Europe, twenty-eight of them in capital cities.

On March 23, 1991, the cities of Austin and Houston, Texas, planned events on the same day. More than twenty thousand believers marched together in the two cities. In August 1991, March for Jesus U.S.A. was established to coordinate the marches springing up across the country as well as to stand with European nations on May 23, 1992. Within six months of forming the necessary office, more than 120 cities had registered to march with believers throughout Europe on the same day.

Many praise marchers have also been captivated by the

hope of marching in sync with believers all over the world on the same day. Plans are forming for June 25, 1994, to be A Day to Change the World. Millions are expected to join in marches for Jesus. Prayer and praise events of every sort will fill the earth. If half of what is planned takes place, there will never have been such a day of praise and prayer in all of history. And many look forward beyond 1994 to even greater occasions for global celebration of Jesus.

A Diverse Movement

As the praise marching comes to life in different communities, it takes on fresh styles and encounters unique difficulties. An event with gigantic throngs numbering tens of thousands requires a great deal of planning. Smaller events can take place with greater spontaneity. Perhaps the smallest on record was three adults, eight children, three banners and a portable tape player.

A few municipalities have initially refused permission for the use of public squares or streets. In some cases, this has merely served to elongate the procession as marchers file along on the sidewalks.

Yet other cities eagerly receive the praise march. The mayor of Lansing, Michigan, had already spoken to a gathering of pastors offering them the keys to the city and welcoming them to "open the gates" and "take the city for Christ." The pastors responded by planning a March for Jesus as the first step.

Diverse styles abound. Many local organizing groups show a flair for innovation and creativity which has strengthened the original concept. For example, the Birmingham, England, organizers have experimented with several different styles of marches. They have tried groups converging from different parts of the city to the center and a march around the city ring road, encircling the city with praise. Marchers were divided up into groups starting at ten different points and covering just over two miles each. Still others have discovered that praise marching makes a suitable entry in local parades and carnival processions.

The hard work to coordinate marches on the same day can be rewarding. In Austin, praise celebrations were also planned to take place in five different prison facilities at nearly the same time as twelve thousand believers rallied elsewhere in the city. The prisoners sang the same songs and prayed for the salvation of their inmates. Lester Haines, who has been in jail ministry for years, said that the presence of God was evident among the prisoners. "It was like the angels were singing with us," he said. Nine inmates received Christ as a result of the marches in the prisons. "They are part of the body of Christ," Haines said, "and it meant a lot to them to participate in this move of God."

Unique to Communities

At times the Spirit of God will direct the prayer themes or routings to touch longstanding needs and deep hurts of the city. Every city has its own unique sites and histories of shame, honor, violence and injustice. Great care is needed to allow Jesus Himself to set the agenda. Many divergent agenda items will inevitably surface when churches combine. If we are marching with Jesus, He will be faithful to make us concerned about what He is concerned about. In some cases we may need to redress an injustice in our city's history. At other times there are personal wounds dealt with that no preset plan could have ever reached.

In Nuremberg, when German Christians marched for

Jesus, it became an act of repentance for the past when that city played host to the great Nazi rallies. For one participant it was also an act of healing:

I was born almost fourteen years before the end of the Third Reich and became a member of Hitler's youth movement, the National Socialist Young People. I was very impressed with the whole concept of the Reich and its origin as well as its beliefs. The two or three big seminars that I went along to shocked and fascinated me at the same time. I found it natural to sing along to the nationalistic songs and raise my right arm as a salutation. The hardships that my family experienced during this time I accepted as a fate which was to be taken with a martyr-like attitude. Later on, however, I came to see it as an unfair and mean device on behalf of the "higher force" (the one above us). That change in attitude came in the summer of 1945 when many things that had been hidden were laid out in the open. I was suspicious of everyone, but especially the youth group. Never again did I want to march with them or take part in a mass meeting.

It would be forty years until I would, after a basic course on Christian belief, once again join a community or a group of people. Eventually I learned to trust and open myself up to people — as I was learning to trust our Lord.

However I still hesitated to go to Nuremberg for a fellowship-retreat, and I tried to think of an excuse not to go on the March for Jesus. The memories of earlier marches, and especially in this city, were too frightening.

It happened differently. Though I carefully planned my schedule so I could miss the march, I found myself free that Sunday. Slightly nervous, I joined the happy crowd. I was surprised that right from the beginning I could march almost without fear, sing along, pray and call out His name. A feeling of freedom grew in me, and I became joyful. I felt like a child in His choir.

As we passed the church where the emperors of the Middle Ages were crowned, our colorful balloons rose up into the sky. With tears in my eyes, I ignored everything around me, only hearing the testimonies and praises to our Lord. When I finally opened my eyes again, I realized, not without shock, that I had lifted my right arm — this time meaning the true salutation (praise to God)!

In other situations, issues no longer exist on a personal scale but have exploded into social unrest. The grievous tensions between Catholics and Protestants in Belfast are a good example. This is how a newspaper in Dublin reported on one March for Jesus:

> Catholics and Protestants marched together, 10,000 strong, through the streets of Dublin last weekend in the March for Jesus. The organizers were leaders from the Republic and Northern Ireland including four priests, four Church of Ireland ministers, Presbyterian and Methodist ministers and lay readers.
>
> Some 1,000 Christians, both Catholic and Protestant, came in coachloads from towns in the North of Ireland, to join in prayer with

people from the Republic...Five Royal Ulster Constabulary officers attending in a private capacity were invited onto the stage to hear organizers tell them they would not be forgotten in the prayers of all those at the rally....

At the GPO building in O'Connell Street, the 3,000 people who have died since the troubles began in Northern Ireland were remembered. In their prayers, the marchers called for an end to sectarianism and violence....

"By doing this," [the organizers explained,] "we want to build friendships across a divide which has existed for too long."

A Roman Catholic lady was asked why she was there marching with Protestants. She replied that she and her husband had come to a personal knowledge of Jesus just a short while before her husband was shot in Belfast. She believed that Jesus was the only answer for them and Ireland. Another Catholic lady commented, "We are all the same at the foot of the cross. Denominations don't count there."

At times the Spirit of God has surprised Christians in a city with an unmistakable prompting to deal with an ancient wound. Black and white pastors planning a praise march in Memphis, Tennessee, wanted to bring attention to Christ's desire for healing of the racial tension in their city. Their first thought was to follow the route of notable protest marches led by Martin Luther King Jr. in an attempt to redeem the tragedy of the turbulent era of the sixties. Upon finding that such a route was not possible, they gave up the idea and simply picked out a convenient location. Only later did they realize that the gathering point they had chosen was the very place where black slaves were auctioned generations ago. Those leaders sensed that God was moving them to get at an even deeper root of bitterness.

Still other times God is pleased to touch the longstanding tensions with a special surge of grace. Doug Hamilton of South Africa reports that a praise march of about seven thousand people made its way through a difficult neighborhood of Johannesburg. The mix of races in the march was remarkable, as they filed past high-rise buildings and windows filled with faces. The wonder, color and joy of their presence shattered the bleak tension of daily life in the city. Without any verbal invitations whatever, people came out from the buildings to join in. In five blocks, up to a hundred joined, many of them expressing a desire simply to participate in the joy.

The presence of worshipping believers can bring the presence of God that can pour healing oil and antiseptic wine into the wounds of a city. Once again, if Christ is the supreme focus, rather than our hurts, the public prayer and praise retain a winsome innocence and power.

A Vision to Be Served

With such a diverse and growing movement, basic service organizations have been needed. Make Way Music in the United Kingdom provided some of the music resources. The March for Jesus U.K. office helped orchestrate the complexity of marching at one time in many places. Coordinators have stepped forward in hundreds of communities to do the really difficult work of encouraging many streams of Christian faith to give joint public praise.

There is certainly no desire to control initiatives of worship but rather to help coordinate cooperative efforts. Tom Pelton of March for Jesus U.S.A. says, "It's not a program we're implementing, but a vision we're serving."

For all the diversity and growth we have seen in praise marching thus far, it is clear that the integral core of the praise march won't ever change: Jesus is worthy of worship. But since we can be distracted from the simplicity of loving God, it is well for leaders of praise marches to act as servant custodians of the simplicity and joy of simply exalting Jesus. Regardless of the benefits and in spite of the opposition and expense, Jesus is worthy of prolonged, devoted public praise.

FIVE

THE HERITAGE OF THE UNWALLED CHURCH

All of us carry into our practice of Christianity a potpourri of assumptions about the nature of it, especially in the expression of its corporateness. These are derived from a variety of sources — upbringing, tradition, exposure to teaching, cultural context, class and political environment, plus factors of personal taste and preference. These assumptions mold practice much more than we may realize. One of these assumptions is that "church" happens behind walls and doors. For millions, a church is conceived as the actual walls and doors. A holy mystique is attached to the physical structure. But, thankfully, more and more Christians are no longer thinking in terms of "going to church" but of the church going to the building, or indeed to the streets.

I was surprised to discover that for the first 250 or so years of its history, the church had no dedicated buildings at all. We should not assume that this was necessarily a conscious policy because persecution, poverty and impermanence make it difficult to own property. In fact, many first-, second- and third-century believers suffered the confiscation of property because of their faith. At the same time, the church in many places was expanding and multiplying. This climate of change contrasts sharply with the atmosphere of static permanence that can attach itself to buildings.

A Triple Imprisonment

Because the church spread with such amazing rapidity and effectiveness across the known world during this period, we should at least question this twentieth-century assumption that a church must have a building. No doubt dedicated buildings can serve a vital purpose and can glorify God both practically and architecturally. On the other hand, they can become a prison, even a beautiful, stained-glass prison, for the church and its message. They can imprison the church physically, hiding the glory which shines out of millions of worshipping faces, keeping the "hands and feet" of Jesus from those who most need His touch and His couriers of good news. Buildings also imprison the church conceptually, perpetuating erroneous assumptions through generations. For instance, the average local church in the Western world has 70 to 150 attendees. Think how easily they can become timid and introspective as they meet over and over again in the same place.

We Christians feel there are not many of us, certainly not enough to effect much change outside these walls. We tend toward defensiveness and a siege mentality. We become suspicious of other Christian groups that are different from us. As we rarely meet them, we are unlikely to dispel or confirm our prejudices. We develop our own "coded" language of worship and spirituality, which in time becomes anachronistic to the outsider. The seating capacity of the building becomes the limit of our faith for growth, or the rows of empty pews produce a constant source of despondency.

We Christians assume that the lost must find us in order to get saved, whereas Jesus came to seek and to save the lost. We forget the one lost sheep outside the fold and busy ourselves with the welfare of the ninety-nine who are safe. Jesus operated the reverse policy. Jesus told us to go into all the world and make disciples. We find it more convenient to stay at home and collect members.

Our imprisonment in buildings can be spiritual as well, insulating us from the people and situations which would otherwise challenge our faith, stir our compassion and lend reality and urgency to our prayers. The salt remains heaped inside the saltshaker. Society, untouched by the spiritual antiseptic of holy lives and active faith, continues to be infected. The spiritual dynamic of worship, which is essentially the manifest presence of God, is confined to the privileged few instead of becoming a testimony and demonstration to the millions in spiritual darkness.

An Event Which Demands an Explanation

On the day of Pentecost when the power of the Holy Spirit was first given to the church, believers were propelled out of a building, not into one. As they came out of the upper room, proclaiming the mighty deeds of God in many tongues, they came face-to-face with a crowd coming in the opposite direction who had heard the sound of the supernatural wind and wanted to know what was going on. We read that the multitude "came together and were bewildered." They "were amazed and marveled." They were full of questions and "continued in amazement and great perplexity, saying to one another, 'What does this mean?' " (Acts 2:5-13).

In response Peter raised his voice and, beginning with an explanation of the phenomena which they were witnessing, preached the first gospel sermon and reaped three thousand souls for the kingdom. Referring to the manifestations of the Spirit of God happening all around he explained, "This is what was spoken of through the prophet Joel" (Acts 2:16).

So much of our evangelism starts in a vacuum and continues in abstract concepts. We have no "this" at which to point. In fact we have to stretch our ingenuity to create a crowd artificially because nothing has happened to cause one to gather. Furthermore, we are answering questions that nobody is asking. Instead of amazement, perplexity and bewilderment, we encounter indifference, apathy and resistance. The church began as an event which demanded an explanation. Consistent with Jesus' own ministry, Pentecost took place in open view and resulted in open mouths and wide eyes!

It is time to recover this ancient heritage and become a city on a hill instead of a lamp hidden beneath a bucket. We must encounter God in full view of the watching world of cities, nations and continents, creating amazement and bewilderment and generating torrents of questions which can be answered with rivers of salvation.

An Ancient Thing Made New

In 1869 a Salvation Army reporter wrote in the organization's paper *The East London Evangelist*:

> We have been much blessed in missioning the streets where the poorest reside. As we go singing down the street...doors fly open and windows shoot up, and soon we have eyes and ears on us from all sides. Every now and then

> we...pause, sing a verse or two, give a short
> address, publishing the glorious gospel...offer
> a few short, earnest prayers; and then go on to
> another corner....

"There is nothing new under the sun," as the world-weary writer of Ecclesiastes commented (Eccl. 1:9, NIV). Worship in the open air is no exception; it has had a place in many phases of church history. Interestingly, this public praise has very often been connected with religious revival.

An early record in England of Christian songs being used outdoors is in 675 A.D. Alfred the Great's handbook records how Aldhelm, the abbot of Malmesbury, decided that, if the people wouldn't come to the message, then the message would come to them. Aldhelm had studied music in Rome. When he returned to Wessex, the people obviously liked the music but had taken to leaving church before the sermon started. As they came out, Aldhelm would be there singing the popular songs of the day, progressing to songs with a Christian message and finally preaching when he'd gathered a crowd!

The medieval monks were the evangelists of their day, and many of them didn't hesitate to use new forms of music in their missions. St. Bernard of Clairvaux (1090-1153) founded his own monastery and was a great church reformer, but he also moved among the common people, preaching, singing and performing signs and wonders in the open fields and town squares. Maybe this timeless hymn he composed was first made popular among peasants in the French countryside:

> Jesus, Thou joy of loving hearts,
> Thou fount of life, Thou light of men,
> From the best bliss which earth imparts,

We turn unfilled to Thee again.

John Hus, leader of a revival movement in the fifteenth century, composed folk hymns in his native Czech for his followers to sing as they met in marketplaces, fields and meadows.

The Catholic and Orthodox churches still continue the tradition of processions in many places today, particularly those associated with pilgrimage. The banners you often see hanging inside Anglican churches were not intended to hang inside the building but to be taken out around the parish. Whit Sunday has always been a time for Christian processions, especially in the Midlands and the North of England.

The idea of taking the gospel out to the people hasn't always met with enthusiasm, even among church leaders. John Wesley was shocked when someone suggested he might preach to the miners of Bristol out in the fields. In his journal on March 31, 1739, Wesley wrote, "I thought the saving of souls almost a sin if it had not been done in a church." He pondered the problem and reflected that Jesus did most of His preaching outdoors. Two days later on April 2 he documented a change in heart: "At four in the afternoon I submitted to be more vile and proclaimed in the highways the glad tidings of salvation." It is sobering to speculate what might have happened to the history of the church in England, and even the fate of the nation, if Wesley had not "submitted to be more vile."

The Salvation Army founded by William Booth took its brass bands onto the streets in the late nineteenth century.[1] They were not always very popular. The *Worthing Gazette* of 1883 described them as "excitable young men and hysterical young women who mistake a quasi-religious revelry for Godliness." At about the same time *Punch* magazine wrote about "Bootheration":

A procession is a nuisance at any time, and should only be permitted on rare and exceptional occasions. As to the noisy Religious Services which disturb the peace and quiet of neighborhoods on the Day of Rest, they should all be confined within the four walls of their own Tabernacle, Camp, Church or Conventicle, whatever it may be, and those walls should be, by Act of Parliament, of sufficient thickness to prevent the escape of noise.

In one twelve-month period 669 Salvationists were assaulted, 56 army buildings were stoned and damaged, and 86 members of the army were jailed by magistrates. But the army grew. In less than ten years it had expanded twenty times over. The army became respected and revered, perhaps because it backed up its noise with a great deal of social concern and action.

One of the Salvation Army's greatest processions was in 1885. It marched to the houses of Parliament with a petition two miles long, bearing 343,000 signatures demanding that the trade in child prostitution (which was rampant at the time) be stopped and the age of consent raised from thirteen to sixteen years old. They succeeded, and lives were changed. Drunkards sobered up and started to care for their families. Prostitutes gave up their ways and turned to respectable employment. Salvation had turned their lives around. A converted coal cart driver summed it up. "Well," he said, "no smoking, no drinking, no swearing, and the 'orses know the difference." The world began to notice the difference too.

General Booth didn't see why the devil should have all the good tunes, and the Salvation Army borrowed them shamelessly. This early Salvationist song goes to the tune of "The Campbells Are Coming."

The Army is coming — amen, amen!
To conquer this city for Jesus — amen!
We'll shout "Hallelujah!" and praise His dear
   name,
Who redeemed us to God through the blood of
   the Lamb.
The sound of its footsteps is rolling along
The kingdom of Satan, triumphant so long,
Is shaking and tott'ring and downward shall
   fall
For Jesus the Savior shall reign over all.

When the Spirit was poured out upon Wales in 1904, society could not escape its impact. For a time the courts had no new cases to try, and the taverns emptied. A report read, "Perhaps the most prominent feature is the lessening of drunkenness, for the night marches (converts on their way home from meetings) of praying and singing converts seem to have induced a considerable number of converts to abandon their evil ways." Another commentator wrote, "The revival of 1904 united denominations as one body, filled the chapels nightly, renewed family ties, changed life in mines and factories, often crowded streets with huge processions, abated social vices and diminished crime."

In more recent times, public praise has surfaced in many parts of the globe. I present the following as random samples as I have not attempted to track these kinds of events worldwide. More than likely some of the best examples have not come to my attention. In fact, I am hoping that this book will stimulate a flow of additional reports for our encouragement. These samples have not been chosen as definitive models but as examples of the variety of public manifestations of the church in recent times and of their geographical diversity.

India

Perhaps the praise marches of greatest size in India were inspired by the Indian church leader Bakht Singh. Early in the 1930s, marches of witness were often a feature of gospel preaching, either to advertise meetings or to touch the powers in pagan situations.

In Madurai, India, the streets of the city are laid out around the great temple of Meenakshi Amman. Their massive walls and towered gates dwarf the houses at their feet. Round and round these streets we marched singing Psalm 24 with such enthusiasm that even Hindus began joining in:

> Lift up your head, O gates!
> And be lifted up, O ancient doors!
> That the King of glory may come in.

On one occasion Bakht Singh gave leadership to what was called a "gospel procession." The children, walking in rows of three, filled up more than a tenth of a mile, he reported. The whole procession was a mile in length with more than ten thousand people taking part, all singing simple hallelujah songs. All the denominations joined in.[2]

China

The well-known Chinese leader Watchman Nee learned of the evangelistic potential of public song early as a high school student. When they were not content with witnessing in the school, the boys carried the gospel out into the town, timing their campaigns for Sundays and festivals and the frequent student strikes. They found a loud and resonant gong, and with it went singing through the streets, proclaiming the good news to all who would pause and listen. The suburbs on both sides of the river became aware of a spiritual awakening among the Christians.[3] Such public proclamation continued on the mainland until it was curtailed by Japanese occupation but blossomed again among Chinese refugees and nationals in Taiwan.

In some churches of Africa, fresh expressions of worship reflect indigenous styles of music and marching that seem ready-made for processional worship. Dean Gilliland, professor of Contextualized Theology and African Studies at Fuller Theological Seminary in Pasadena, California, told me of such an innovation of worship in a Catholic church in Cameroon in 1968.

Catholic churches experienced a refreshing of some worship forms in the late 1960s. In the city of Yaounde the early mass would be announced around the city by a drummer. In pied-piper fashion the drummer wound his way through the city, picking up worshippers as he went. In single file, somewhat unorganized, the line of singing and dancing marchers would get longer and louder. About three hundred people, young and old, would be "picked up" on the streets of the city and come to the mass at the cathedral.

Reports abound of other African churches enjoying public processions of praise.

During the sixties, several large parades of testimony were organized throughout Latin America with the help of the Latin American Mission. One of the most memorable took place in Guatemala in 1962.[4] A gigantic evangelical parade and rally climaxed a nationwide evangelistic effort right in the midst of a revolution attempting to overthrow the government.

Even as plans were being set in motion on the day of the parade, fighting broke out in the city. The rat-a-tat of machine guns and the buzz of diving fighter planes shattered the atmosphere. A plane was shot down. The president's mansion was attacked as a group of military officers staged a rebellion. All the carefully laid plans for the march went into utter confusion.

Hundreds of buses were already converging on the capital from all directions. Twenty-eight floats were ready. Signs were painted and mounted on wooden frames. "If I get lost" cards were pinned on little children. Thousands of maps showing order and formation had been distributed days before. This parade was to have been a magnificent testimony to the entire city, the entire nation.

But these Christian believers from all over the country were determined to give public witness to their faith in Christ. Thirty thousand people came to march over the twenty-six-block route in spite of the chaos and an intermittent rain. It was a strange mixture — beautiful floats and humble, bare-footed Indian mothers carrying their babies; well-dressed, middle-class believers and those in tattered clothes; smiling women and children and grim-faced men and grandfathers. As the day progressed, the revolt was halted, and President Miguel Ydigoras Fuentes, under heavy guard, came to the rally in the Olympic Stadium.

Afterward, thousands of Christians began the long trek homeward, many of them to isolated villages scattered throughout the mountains, but they were rejoicing because they no longer stood alone. They had experienced the thrill of being united with thirty thousand fellow believers.

The people of Guatemala have not forgotten the splendor of public praise. In 1982, over hundreds of thousands of believers made their way from all points of the country to the capital in singing processions. Christians were guided en route by helicopter and radio links. Over 700,000 converged at a rally where the gospel was proclaimed. They celebrated the centennial of the arrival of evangelical missionaries as well as the sending of their own.

God has stirred His church to give abundant public testimony to the joy of knowing Him in many generations, with many styles and at widespread places.

The Heritage Has a Future

Believers today can rejoice doubly: Their public praise follows a rich heritage of a witnessing church. But it is exhilarating to consider how that very heritage extends to a brilliant future of extravagant public praise among the nations.

It doesn't seem at all that incredible to hear of plans to organize an expression of public praise in every nation as soon as 1994. Some eager worshippers view all that has gone before as a mere rehearsal for what could be the world's most massive celebration of Jesus yet, to take place in the year A.D. 2000.

And why not expect great things of public worship? As the sheer number of believers now grows the world over, surely we can expect an increasing overflow of witness. In some places, new believers multiply at rates outstripping any sensible efforts to house them in church buildings. And though there is no doubt that to give public testimony will come at great cost to believers where the gospel is opposed, is it not likely that some of the greatest outbreaks of public worship might come forth in Asia or Africa or Latin America?

SIX

THE BATTLE
FOR WORSHIP

And the whole earth was amazed and followed
after the beast; and they worshiped the dragon,
because he gave his authority to the beast; and
they worshiped the beast, saying, "Who is like
the beast, and who is able to wage war with
him?" (Rev. 13:3-4).

When the nature of Satan's kingdom is brought
to light, there is no doubt about what Satan
desires from the human race: that which belongs to God — our worship. As the apocalyptic visions
of Revelation unfold, a stark choice is offered to the
inhabitants of the earth: worship the dragon and the beast,
or worship the Lamb of God. They either have their hands
or foreheads stamped with the 666 mark of subservience
to the prince of darkness, or they let the gentle hand of
Jesus write there His name and the name of His Father.
They choose either to sing, "Who is like the beast?" or
"Salvation to our God who sits on the throne, and to the
Lamb" (Rev. 7:10). The final battle is essentially a battle
for worship, and both armies are enlisting soldiers for the
fight.

With the current interest in spiritual warfare has come
the discovery that there is power in praise and worship.
Though power is released when we worship, it is impor-

tant to understand that worship is not so much a weapon as it is the very prize of the battle. "Fear God, and give Him glory, because the hour of His judgment has come; and worship Him who made the heaven and the earth and sea and springs of waters" (Rev. 14:7). The Father is seeking worshippers upon whom to lavish His affection for eternity. The deceiver is seeking victims whose capacity for worship he will mercilessly plunder only to plunge them headlong into his own inevitable spiral of destruction.

Worship is a heavenly activity exported to the earth. It predates human vocal chords, for the Bible says at the creation of the world, "The morning stars sang together and all the angels shouted for joy" (Job 38:7, NIV). Prophets saw through the eyes of the Spirit into the throne room of the eternal God and glimpsed scenes of breathtaking worship. Glorious beings of terrifying power and beauty sang praises, augmented by choirs of innumerable angels. Alive with supernatural music and vibrant with the sights and sounds of pure and total devotion, heaven's preoccupation has always been and ever will be the greatness and glory of the living God. When His kingdom comes and His will is done on earth as it is in heaven, it will begin with an invasion of worship — heaven's highest activity.

When people on earth become preoccupied with the Person of God, when they encounter His mercy, His grace and His love, they naturally sing. This heavenly activity breaks out and collides with an opposite kingdom on earth where worship has long since been diverted, perverted and squandered upon the creature rather than the Creator. Worship is at the heart of a conflict of kingdoms.

The Fall of the Anointed Cherub

The Lord had created many stupendous beings to fill His courts with praise and to carry out His purposes. Among these was Lucifer, the son of the morning, perhaps the most glorious and powerful. "You had the seal of perfection, full of wisdom and perfect in beauty. You were in Eden, the garden of God; every precious stone was your covering...You were the anointed cherub who covers, and I placed you there. You were on the holy mountain of God; you walked in the midst of the stones of fire. You were blameless in your ways from the day you were created" (Ezek. 28:12b-15).

Billy Graham in his book *Angels* comments, "He was the most brilliant and most beautiful of all created beings in heaven. He was probably the ruling prince of the universe under God."[1] Yet this incredible being, created for the glory of God, shifted his gaze to himself. "Your heart was lifted up because of your beauty; you corrupted your wisdom by reason of your splendor. I cast you to the ground" (Ezek. 28:17).

Again Isaiah describes this terrible insurrection. "How you have fallen from heaven, O star of the morning, son of the dawn!...You said in your heart, 'I will ascend to heaven; I will raise my throne above the stars of God...I will ascend above the heights of the clouds; I will make myself like the Most High' " (Is. 14:12-14).

Not content to be the most glorious of the worshippers, leading the whole celestial population in extravagant praise of the Most High, Lucifer is consumed by pride and covets the throne where heaven's worship is received. He recruits perhaps a third of the angels to his cause (Rev. 12:4). War breaks out, and the rebels are thrown down to the earth to aid and abet their new master in his pursuit of personal power and glory, collaborators in his lust to be the center of his own twisted universe.

Worship is a fundamental expression of character. Worship is the difference between the "I wills" of Satan as he coveted the throne and the "not My will, Father, but Yours" of Jesus as He surrendered to the cross. In essence these are the two battle songs of the two kingdoms. We choose to sing one or the other.

A closer study of these texts about the history of evil reveals a fascinating possibility about the role of Lucifer within his original calling. In describing Lucifer, Ezekiel first enumerates the precious stones of his covering, implying a priestly role. Then he describes the workmanship of Lucifer's "settings and sockets" (Ezek. 28:13). Most translations carry in their margins the alternative translations of "tambourines and flutes" or "tabrets and pipes." It seems that Lucifer himself had the capacity to create heavenly music! He may have been the one who created celestial symphonies to lead the whole company of heaven in processions of praise for the eternal King. This is a sober reminder for those who lead public praise marches to focus the attention on Jesus and not on themselves.

So we see Satan as an "anointed cherub," dressed in the manner of a priest (by virtue of his jewelled covering which is consistent with the typology of the Bible). His ministry was "covering the throne of God" in the "mountain of God," a kind of heavenly worship leader (see Ezek. 28:14-15). He filled the highest place of all with music of unimaginable splendor as would only befit the Ancient of Days in His majesty. Then we see him fall, corrupted and spoiled, ejected from the holy of holies.

There is no evidence that he was stripped of his wisdom and splendor when he fell or that he forfeited the abilities he was given when he was created. How could he make war in heaven if his power was gone? In fact, although he lost his place, he did not lose his power. In his fall to earth he brought with him all his abilities, except that now they served the profane purposes of his corrupted personality. The glory of his appearance became a cloak to hide his evil nature. We could reasonably argue that his priestly anointing for worship in all its supernatural power with its musical accompaniment is now employed for a new purpose: to capture the hearts, minds and wills of the inhabitants of the place where he fell — the people of the earth.

Fighting for the Prize

Scholars tell us that nearly all primitive people of the earth believe that music was of divine origin. Every civilization has some kind of legend concerning the origin and creation of music. In practically every case, a god discovers it and passes it on to mankind. From earliest times music was used exclusively for worship, whether of idols, demons or the true God. All tribes, however primitive, had musical instruments of some kind.

Music and worship are inextricably linked in every culture. Where a secular society denies the spiritual dimension, music continues to be used to express devotion to ideologies, causes, pleasure, material possessions and so on. We all know that music has power to inspire, to soothe, to invite us to dance or to sleep. It can slip through the mind's defenses and reach the spirit with a language more subtle than words. In itself it is neither good nor evil, but it has power that can be employed for either end.

While Lucifer, now Satan, prowls the earth like a roaring lion looking for someone to devour, Jesus calls us to harmonize with heaven, to move in rhythmic step with His angel armies and drown out the discordant orchestras of hell with ever-increasing crescendos of praise.

Against this background it seems natural to discover worship center stage in the theater of spiritual warfare. Every war is fought in order to possess something or to avoid losing it — whether wealth, power, glory or ideologies. Satan is fighting for the adulation and servitude of the human race. Satan's war is for possession of all that God created for His glory and pleasure. The crown of that creation is the human race, every person uniquely made, capable of fellowship with his or her Maker, made for worship.

When Lucifer fell to earth he found it already inhabited. In fact it was more than inhabited. It was governed. God gave the right of rulership to the people He had created and had given the breath of life. Despite all his power of heavenly origin, Lucifer was impotent to take the control he wanted. He had to employ other and more cunning means.

Thus Satan did not make his debut upon the earth as a magnificent, overwhelmingly powerful angelic being, but he took the form of a creature, a slimy serpent. The serpent clearly does not exercise power over Adam and Eve but appears to find itself, along with all the other creatures, subject to their authority. As a result, his attack is via the subtlety of deception.

Satan had power but no kingdom on earth in which to exercise it. He had to find a power base. In order to gain any kind of authority in the world of mankind, Satan had to do it through those who had already been given authority. He knew that the only way he could get it was if he caused them to compromise that authority in the only way they could — disobedience to God resulting in sin.

Therefore his method of attack was for Eve, as it is for us, through the mind. He works through the subtlety of suggestion, "Did God really say...?" and the exploitation of a tempting idea, "when you eat of it your eyes will be opened" (see Gen. 3:1,4, NIV). He used no weapon but ideas and had no battleground but the human mind. It was enough.

Satan extends his power base by propagating ideas, by deceit, by lies, by temptation. If music can serve his cause, he will employ it to the extreme.

The Heart of the Battle

The history of the battle for worship is an ancient one. One of the earliest victories of God prefigured all that would follow. At the Exodus God did not merely demand that evildoers "let my people go." He released the people so that "they may worship me" (Ex. 8:1, NIV).

The first global display of God's triumph over the gods of this world (Ex. 12:12; 15:11; 18:11) was marked by song and the procession of the people He had brought to Himself to serve Him as priests (Ex. 19:4-6).

That first song of God's people, the song of Moses, is a victory celebration of God over His enemies (Ex. 15:1-18). That very song of Moses finds abundant reprise in the last days as Revelation 15 declares. At that point those who are victorious in God declare that all nations will join in pilgrimage procession to worship God fully (Rev. 15:2-8). The temple stands open as if in anticipation of their arrival. And, indeed, the nations do come in continual worship (Rev. 21:24-26).

The point is not so much that Satan has been granted great musical powers, although that is likely, or that saints now wage war somehow in their coming to God to worship, although that is clear as well. The point is simply that the goal of the entire struggle is for the worship of humanity. If we steadfastly worship God, the heart of the battle is won.

This became clear to me years ago in my early days of

exploring the concept of the praise march. In studying the famous story of Joshua at Jericho, I saw something I had not seen before. Central to the story is the encounter between two captains, Joshua's army and the One who introduced himself as the "captain of the host of the Lord" (see Josh. 5:14).

Joshua had perhaps been deep in thought and suddenly became aware of an army intruder. Suddenly alert and on his guard, Joshua steps forward with the challenge, "Are you for us or for our enemies?" "Neither," was the reply, "but as commander of the army of the Lord I have now come" (Josh. 5:13-14, NIV). Joshua bowed low in worship before him, inquiring if there was any message. No doubt Joshua was eager to position his army to be in sync with the efforts of the unseen angelic army of God. But the instructions were simply to worship more extensively by removing his sandals.

Joshua received more than a mere strategy. He received a promise of victory: "See, I have given Jericho into your hand" (Josh. 6:2). In the moment that Joshua worshipped, the outcome of the battle was decided. Once Joshua had fallen before Jesus, Jericho was certain to fall before Joshua.

How wonderful to consider that there is glorious synchronization, a glorious coalition of heavenly and earthly forces under one captain. However conscious we may become of a supernatural dimension as we encircle our own Jerichos, we only need to see the captain, worship Him, obey Him and follow Him.

The war for worship becomes clear as we consider the triumph of Jesus in the same battle every person has faced. As Jesus emerged the victor in every temptation put before Him, perhaps the final one is most telling. The devil offered Jesus all the kingdoms of earth and their glory if Jesus would offer to Satan a small, perhaps even momentary, gesture of worship. You know the story: Jesus not only refused but quoted Scripture verses declaring God's ancient purpose to be the sole recipient of worship (see Luke 4:8).

If Jesus won the battle for worship, so can we. He has made a way for us in Himself. No one has been baited with so high a bounty by Satan. Yet Jesus remained in abject, utter devotion to His Father. If Jesus won this skirmish, surely we can be confident that He will gain the desire of His Father, that the kingdoms of the world and their glory would be turned to God.

SEVEN

MARCHING WITH JESUS

Rejoice greatly, O daughter of Zion!...
Behold, your king is coming to you;...
Humble, and mounted on a donkey,
Even on a colt, the foal of a donkey.

Zechariah 9:9

Without doubt the event which has come to be known as Palm Sunday or the triumphal entry was the most public act of Jesus' ministry. Much that He said and did in the rest of His ministry had the effect of thinning crowds, not winning them. But on this extraordinary occasion the biblical writers show Jesus as the organizer of a visible event. He had made His destination known for weeks ahead of time. His launching point was where He had performed His most amazing miracle, raising Lazarus from the dead. He sent two disciples on ahead to make ready the unbroken colt. A momentum had been building as He toured the country, collecting followers as He went, His face set "like flint" toward Jerusalem (Is. 50:7). He seemed to have planned what was necessary, and when the spontaneous praise broke out, He refused to restrain it.

Yet this climactic act seems to have become eclipsed by our focus on the more somber dramas of betrayal, arrest and crucifixion and the glorious triumph of resurrection and ascension which follows. Of course, preachers often exaggerate the problem by suggesting that the people in the exuberant crowd became the mob who condemned Christ before Pilate a few days later. This is at best speculation and at worst has the effect of making the hearers suspicious of drawing too much inspiration from the event.

It remains true that Jesus planned and prepared for the triumphal entry, entered fully into it, knew that it was a fulfillment of ancient prophecy and refused to receive any criticism over it. That should be more than enough reason for us to look deeply into its significance.

For no reason that I can identify, this story did not figure greatly in my conscious development of thought around marching for Jesus or the molding of the practice. Despite its obvious similarities, I am not aware that any of us attempted to use the triumphal entry as a model. Yet with one eye on the Gospel accounts and the other on the past six years, I am surprised at how many similarities I see.

I must be quick to point out that this is not an attempt to justify a contemporary recreation of Palm Sunday. It was a unique, one-time historical event that cannot be reconstructed. An attempt to recreate it might have some value as a piece of biblical drama or visual aid for teaching but probably nothing more.

The triumphal entry fulfilled Zechariah's prophecy, and it can be a foreshadowing of what is still to come. However, in no way do contemporary praise marchers profess to be acting out a fulfillment of this prophecy. Our desire is to have a part in all that Jesus prepared for every generation of His disciples. A praise march opens up an avenue of worship for all those whose hearts are bursting with hosannas.

So let us begin to understand praise marches today by revisiting the Gospel accounts and thrilling to this timeless story, beginning in Jericho, where momentum was gathering.

Expecting Miracles

> And as they were going out from Jericho, a great multitude followed Him. And behold, two blind men sitting by the road, hearing that Jesus was passing by, cried out, saying, "Lord, have mercy on us, Son of David!" (Matt. 20:29-30).

Jesus was on His way to Jerusalem accompanied by a growing mass of the common people. In His sights was the capital city, the seat of power and authority, the symbol of nationhood, the stage upon which thousands of years of turbulent history had been played out. Most poignantly of all, Jerusalem would be the setting for His own imminent passion.

For the ragged multitude of the poor and powerless who enthusiastically blocked the streets and disrupted the daily business of Jericho, their Messiah had arrived. The nearer He led them toward Jerusalem, the more a coronation seemed possible and with it, perhaps, their deliverance from their oppressors, both military and religious.

Intoxicated by miracles, with dreams of a new order and a deliverer, the cries of two blind beggars by the side of the road came as an interruption, and the crowds sternly quieted them. But it was for the sake of such outcasts that Jesus was going to Jerusalem, and so the momentum of this great procession was halted and magnetized to the spot where Jesus stopped to ask, "What do you want Me to do for you?" (v. 32). When they asked for healing, Jesus was moved with compassion and touched their eyes. Immediately they received their sight and followed Him.

In the midst of the noise, joy and hope that fill the streets when we follow our Messiah toward the heavenly Jerusalem, Jesus is listening for cries for mercy. So must we. In our invasion of the streets, if we are truly the body of Christ, then Jesus is truly passing by. In His compassion Christ is ready to respond to cries for mercy, if we are ready to reach out in His name.

The only way in which countless desperate people are going to know the touch of Christ is if they "hear him passing by." The only way in which Jesus can pass by today is through the body of Christ, the church which has inherited His anointing to "bring good news to the afflicted" (Is. 61:1). Shut away in special buildings, often barricaded by cultural irrelevance and "coded" language, the church is the hardest to reach for those who need Him the most.

Some have criticized marching for Jesus as being triumphalistic, mistaking it as a parade of the more victorious features of the Christian faith to the neglect of compassion for those who suffer. It seems that some on the streets of Jericho thoughtlessly tried to silence cries for mercy, and this must be taken as a warning to us. But joyful celebration of Jesus and a response to those who cry out were not in conflict in Jesus' march.

The noise of the excitement surrounding Jesus may have been the very means by which the faith of the blind men was excited. After all, their petition was triggered by hearing that Jesus was passing by. Even then Jesus did not chide the noisy crowd and call for two minutes of silent sympathy for the sufferers. He was moved with compassion, and His compassion manifested itself in healing power as He touched their eyes. "Immediately they received their sight and followed Him." From that point on, those two probably out-triumphed any triumphalists as they continued toward the Holy City!

As we march, we must move in step with Jesus' heart of compassion and pray that compassion will give rise to much more than sympathy when the deepest cry is for healing. Here it is important to remember that whereas a public praise march may only take place on a special occasion, it takes place in the context of the other 364 days of the year. During those days Christ's compassion and power can be ministered without limit through those who are obedient.

During my first attempt at writing songs for the streets, the hope and longing for seeing outbreaks of healing as we worshipped gripped my imagination.

The song I wrote took the form of an announcement of Christ's kingdom beginning with the proclamation, "We declare that the kingdom of God is here." As I write this book the incidents of healing in the context of street praise are quite common but far short of what I dreamed of. Nevertheless, I believe they are precious tokens of what will become a much greater outbreak in the future.

Even as Jesus began the march with healing the blind beggars, the culmination of His march at the temple was graced by miracles. By that time in all likelihood a stream of people was seeking healing, for we read in Matthew 21:14, "And the blind and the lame came to Him in the temple, and He healed them."

Perhaps the beautiful outbreaks of healing which can punctuate a "Jesus procession" in our day are a prelude to a time when in the temple made of living stones, whether in streets, houses, church buildings or stadiums, multitudes will stream in and find healing just as surely as they did in the temple of Jesus' day.

Those whom Jesus had healed did not have to wait until

the next Sabbath to find a context in which to apply their newfound faith and express their joy. They were already "in church," and church was a procession of praise.

A God-ward Celebration

One of the most beautiful features of a procession arises out of its very nature. A crowd gathered in a building with seats and aisles quickly becomes static. A curious outsider has little choice but to become a passive observer. Too easily a lack of movement becomes synonymous with sacredness, hushed voices with holiness and spirituality with spectatorism as the performance of the few on the platform occupies the rapt (or not!) attention of the many in the pews. The nature of a march is entirely different. It is a riot of movement and color, a smiling parade of humanity in all its shapes and sizes, ages and conditions, and it is going somewhere. Not that a regular church meeting is not necessary or does not have its place, but what better way to symbolize a people movement than by moving people! And what better picture of a call to God than the one Jesus most often used, "Follow Me." I well remember a photo of the extreme back end of the City march in 1987. A wise-guy group of Christians had draped a large banner over their shoulders proclaiming, "Jesus said, 'Follow Me!' "

Many marches have been reported as growing considerably along the route. Mostly this has been by way of other believers getting caught up in it, but frequently it is the curious or the spiritually hungry. When fifty-five thousand of us were marching between the houses of Parliament and Hyde Park in London, a homeless young man was attracted by the sight and somehow got drawn along. Marchers befriended him, sharing their sandwiches and their faith as they picnicked at the march's end. He couldn't get work without a place to live and couldn't get a place to live without work. Members of our church found him a place in a hostel run by one of our churches. There he found a personal relationship with the Jesus for whom we had all been marching. He began by following us and ended up following Jesus.

A march is not a march without participation. Again, this is a graphic illustration to the outsider that church is not a performance like the movies or the theater, but the sum total of many individuals' commitment to follow Jesus. There is a glorious variety of individuals but no stubborn individualism, for all have chosen to move in the same direction, not only because they love to be together, but because they are all following the same Person.

The very manner of Jesus' arrival at the great city is itself a powerful picture of the nature of His government. This King breaks all the rules and comes humbly, not a bodyguard in sight. To some He may even have appeared ridiculous, but His glory is in His meekness. His magnificence is in His unself-conscious vulnerability.

He is not on a war horse because His battle will not be with foes of flesh and blood. He comes not to subject the people, writing His laws in their blood, but to set them free from their subjection, writing a new law of grace in His own blood. Even the most timid of those who try to get near Him will not be intimidated by the slow but steady approach of His donkey as they might be by the prancing strength and stature of a great stallion.

Certainly the children found much in His procession to endear them to Him. The One who came to carry our burdens chooses a beast of burden and makes it easy for the weak to come near. As ever, Jesus is travelling light and has not so much as a saddle. Yet His foregoing of even this small comfort and privilege becomes an opportunity for the common people to participate. They seize the coats off their own backs and improvise both a saddle and a highway in His honor. In this moment of adulation, the spoiling of their clothes was of little interest as they gladly laid them down in a spontaneous gesture of devotion.

We can learn much from this scene if we are desirous of marching in the same manner as Jesus did. There is a striking contrast to the marches of other kingdoms. The raw threat of a thousand jackboots mechanically stabs the air, followed by enough military hardware to fry a planet, the anarchic frenzy of the mob, the belligerent chanting of a political rally, the pride and pomp of royal cavalcades, the lawlessness and licentiousness of Mardi Gras parades and so on. If, however, we want to march with Jesus, we must share in the character of His kind of march. We will find that its nature is determined by His character.

Luke reports, "The whole multitude of the disciples began to praise God joyfully with a loud voice for all the miracles which they had seen" (Luke 19:37). Above all, a public praise march is a celebration of God, to God. There was a spontaneity and creativity as they borrowed songs and symbols from a variety of festivals, from coronation parades and the holy day feasts of Israel, but it all flew heavenward. Similarly a March for Jesus is not a protest march. It is not focused on an issue, however valid. Despite its potential for displacing spiritual powers of darkness, it is not focused on them, but upon the One in whose name demons flee. It is not focused on the onlookers though they are acknowledged and invited to give glory to God also. Finally, it is not focused on the participants, though we thrill to see His glory reflected in the faces of others as we fix our eyes on Jesus.

Jesus' procession did not take place in a vacuum. It

started with a momentum of miracles which had peaked in the stupendous raising of Lazarus from the dead. The whole multitude of the disciples took up the acclamation, conceivably as a chant, "Blessed is the King who comes in the name of the Lord; peace in heaven and glory in the highest!" (Luke 19:38). Similarly, contemporary praise processions do not happen in a vacuum. They become a festive moment to heap heavenward ten thousand times ten thousand thanksgivings for all the miracles of grace, great and small, that the participants have seen God perform in their lives. The focus for this and the catalyst of it is Jesus Himself, the One through whom the goodness of God comes to us and through whom our thanksgiving is received in heaven. The disciples' shouts of praise looked backward on what God had done but more so looked forward in anticipation of what was yet to come.

A Global Invitation

This God-ward festive thankfulness was not without its precedent in various processions of Israel. There was a standing order to "enter His gates with thanksgiving and His courts with praise" (Ps. 100:4, NIV). But this exhortation is not directed only to the few. The psalm begins, "Shout joyfully to the Lord, all the earth" (v. 1). As the world looks on, our own expressions of thankfulness are an invitation and exhortation to them to join the procession as it winds its way toward the temple, the "house of prayer for all the nations" (Mark 11:17). When King David had brought the ark of the covenant into Zion, he established an era of extravagant and continual praise. "David first assigned Asaph and his relatives to give thanks to the Lord" (1 Chron. 16:7). They sang a song of thanksgiving: "Oh give thanks to the Lord, call upon His name; make known His deeds among the peoples...Sing to the Lord, all the earth...Ascribe to the Lord, O families of the peoples, ascribe to the Lord glory and strength. Ascribe to the Lord the glory due His name; bring an offering, and come before Him" (1 Chron 16:8,23,28,29).

The last few stanzas of David's inaugural song are "Oh give thanks to the Lord, for He is good; for His lovingkindness is everlasting." These words reappear in a dramatic context under a later king, Jehoshaphat. It seems an unlikely song to sing for a Levite choir leading the army against overwhelming odds. Though on a human level it was a foolish suicide mission, "when they began singing and praising, the Lord set ambushes against the sons of Ammon, Moab, and Mount Seir, who had come against Judah; so they were routed" (2 Chron. 20:22). As they gave thanks, choosing to be absorbed with the lovingkindness of God instead of the enemy or their own fate, He dealt with their enemies.

There is something utterly fundamental about giving thanks to God, something which confronts the spirit of the age in which we live. Paul refers to the attitude of sinful humanity from the beginning who, "though they knew God, they did not honor Him as God, or give thanks" (Rom. 1:21). Public thanksgiving flies dramatically in the face of the pride, cynicism and arrogant self-reliance of this world's kingdoms. Perhaps those unearthly champions of praise, the angelic hosts, fly with it.

> Blessed is He who comes in the name of the
> Lord;
> Blessed is the coming kingdom of our father
> David;
> Hosanna in the highest!
>   Mark 11:9-10

This bold acclamation which the milling disciples took up was not a random choice or a spontaneous invention. They began with a direct quotation from Psalm 118, a psalm that was sung at all great festivals, including the one to which they were going (see Ps. 118:26). Interestingly, the psalm begins and ends with the familiar refrain, "Give thanks to the Lord, for He is good; for His lovingkindness is everlasting." It also contains the prophecy about the stone which the builders rejected becoming the chief cornerstone, a passage packed with Messianic significance. Jesus applied that Scripture verse to Himself only days later in His controversies with the religious leaders in the temple.

So for the crowd there was no doubt: they were welcoming *a* Messiah, if not *the* Messiah, a position to which some of the Pharisees vehemently objected. Though the crowd understood little about the nature of Jesus' kingdom, He never once corrected or attempted to silence them. When the Pharisees criticized the crowd, Jesus supported the excitement of the people, explaining that if they were silent, the stones would cry out in their place (Luke 19:39-40).

With their words His people not only bless Him and proclaim Him King but also attribute to Him the credentials of coming in the name of the Lord, carrying the full authority and approval of Almighty God behind Him. Having blessed the King, they then bless the coming kingdom of our father David with joyful anticipation.

The fundamental dynamic demonstrated here is once again the very same one which I believe provides the highest motive and deepest integrity to public praise today. It is an adoring focus on the Person at the center of it all, the one who "comes in the name of the Lord," Jesus, the King of the nations. With this simple motive hundreds of thousands of ordinary believers are "voting with their feet" in an increasing number of marches.

It must be said, however, that for many, perhaps leaders in particular, the "worship Jesus" motive has at first seemed too simple or not enough to justify all the effort involved. Those who live in goal-oriented cultures habitually measure the value of an event by the discernible product of it. They ask, for example, how many came, how many inquired, how many got converted, how many supporters signed up, how much was the offering and so on. While these factors are important, we risk measuring success by the wrong criteria. First of all, in the kingdom of God there is no success or failure, only obedience. So if we march in obedience to the Spirit of God, His approval is our success, whether we gain people or lose them, whether we cover our costs or make a loss, whether people congratulate or criticize us.

We would be in serious trouble if we measured our human love relationships by a series of statistics. What a tragedy it would be to cheapen the love relationship between Christ and His bride, the church, in the same way. Think about Mary's extravagant anointing of Jesus at Bethany, which John says occurred on the eve of Palm Sunday. Who objected to the "waste" of the fine ointment? Judas. Jesus defended Mary and received the anointing — in all its apparent wastefulness — as a precious act of extravagant worship (see John 12:3-8). If we are stirred by the Spirit of God to anoint Jesus publicly with adoration in the form of a praise march, then let us do it because we want to bless the King who comes in the name of the Lord.

By all means we can gather evidence of God's blessing in measurable ways if we wish. But surely this, like the fragrance which filled the house where the anointing took place, is but the overspill of the central act of worship which flowed from an adoring heart. If you are looking for converts to count, I suspect that where extravagant love for Jesus is being demonstrated, you will find them anyway.

An Overflow of Joy

I have long believed that the redeemed company of God's people should be the happiest people on earth. This is not to deny the suffering and rejection that Jesus promised would come to those who desire to be like Him. Yet countless saints through the ages have found that a quality of heavenly joy breaks through at such times. Even Jesus, for the joy that was set before Him, endured the cross, despising its shame. I long for the time when the world looks at the people of God and longs desperately to taste the joy they see in us, when the sheer happiness of Christ's worshippers engenders within others a hunger to know Him too.

Psalm 40 traces a standard sequence of salvation that spills gloriously over into the world:

> I waited patiently for the Lord;
> And He inclined to me, and heard my cry.
> He brought me up out of the pit of destruction,
>   out of the miry clay;
> And He set my feet upon a rock making my
>   footsteps firm.
> And He put a new song in my mouth, a song
>   of praise to our God;
> Many will see and fear,
> And will trust in the Lord.
>
> Psalm 40:1-3

How is it that the public imagines a Christian as someone somber, censorious and colorless. Undoubtedly, the deceiver has long been operating his propaganda machine to this effect, but admittedly we have provided him with plenty of source material. Clearly the psalmist is not hiding his joyful song of praise. As a result many will see, and in seeing they will fear. The "fear of the Lord" and the awe come when a person is exposed to His holy presence. But the testimony of the singer also bears witness to a God of mercy, grace and forgiveness, and the hearer gains confidence to put his trust in the Lord.

Similarly, in King David's psalm of repentance he cries out, "Restore to me the joy of Thy salvation, and sustain me with a willing spirit. Then I will teach transgressors Thy ways, and sinners will be converted to Thee" (Ps. 51:12-13). We need to hit back at Satan's propaganda campaign and break the popular caricatures of dullness and joylessness by letting the joy of Christ's salvation spill onto the streets. From the earliest Make Way marches, we encouraged participants not to hide their joy but to feel free to dress colorfully — some even donned clown costumes. They carried banners and balloons, threw candies to children, smiled and, of course, sang the songs and shouted the joyful shouts. As a result, others have noticed the march, found themselves in awe of God's presence and put their trust in Him.

A Harmony of Joy and Tears

He saw the city, and wept over it (Luke 19:41).

The triumphal entry of Jesus was held together in perfect harmony in a surprising diversity of emotion. From Jericho to Jerusalem the route was distinguished not only with festivity but also with deep compassion for the sick, the amazed yelps of the newly healed, the joyful praises of the children, the scowling indignation of the Pharisees. Jesus' heart broke as He looked out over the city and foresaw the dreadful reward of its unrepentant will. He burned with anger as He drove out the money changers at the temple.

Some have criticized praise marches on the grounds that the unrepentant state of our city populations requires mourning rather than dancing, the sackcloth and ashes of repentance rather than the joy of our salvation. However, walking in Jesus' footsteps during His earthly ministry would tell a bigger story. Joy and tears existed side by side in Jesus' procession, and so they can in the procession of His church today. During His descent from the Mount of Olives, as the metropolis of Jerusalem lay spread before Him, Jesus wept in the midst of the rejoicing crowd (Luke 19:41).

Weeping Over Cities

To Him Jerusalem was a familiar sight, more full of significance and pathos than we can possibly imagine. He had come to Jerusalem year after year to celebrate the feasts of Israel in the company of relatives and friends. At the age of twelve He had absconded to the temple and been found "about his Father's business," debating with the scholars there. Jerusalem was the evocative symbol of a nation chosen by God yet apostate and under judgment, its gates, walls and turrets echoing with centuries of turbulent history. However, sentiment did not cause His weeping but a deeply disturbing vision of future judgment, grief over the consequences of their blindness.

If you had known in this day, even you, the things which make for peace! But now they have been hidden from your eyes. For the days shall come upon you when your enemies will throw up a bank before you, and surround you, and hem you in on every side, and will level you to the ground and your children within you, and they will not leave in you one stone upon another, because you did not recognize the time of your visitation (Luke 19:42-44).

Jesus' prophecy was graphically fulfilled in A.D. 70 when the Romans, under Emperor Titus, besieged the city, took it and proceeded to level it to the ground, slaughtering its inhabitants mercilessly.

If our desire is to "march with Jesus" today, what lessons can we take from Jesus' prophecy over Jerusalem? First of all, let us not all rush to be prophets of doom over our cities. Jesus was indeed pronouncing judgment, but He was not judgmental in His attitude. Guard against that self-righteous element that lurks in the gloomier corners of the church and delights in pronouncing doom! His tender love qualified Jesus to say what He said, love even for those He knew were about to do away with Him.

The incident is very similar to one Luke reports when Jesus cries out, "O Jerusalem, Jerusalem, the city that kills the prophets and stones those sent to her! How often I wanted to gather your children together, just as a hen gathers her brood under her wings, and you would not have it!" (Luke 13:34). Jesus' tears over the city were not a shallow, passing emotion but the overflow of years of longing for them to be saved, even though they neither recognized Him nor came to Him.

Jesus still weeps over cities with a longing for their salvation and grief where He sees their judgment coming. We must learn to weep with Him, entering into His longings for their inhabitants. Even in the midst of joyful celebration we can expect to feel our hearts mourning with the great heart of the One who "is not willing that any should perish but that all should come to repentance."

Though they long for God, there are multitudes who will not or cannot cry out to God for themselves. For the second Make Way march, I wrote a chorus to address this problem. I hoped that God might graciously fill it with substance as people took it upon their lips on the streets.

> Lord, have mercy on this nation
> For the sake of Jesus Christ.
> Cleanse us, heal us, save us
> For the sake of Jesus Christ.

I received the following report about the singing of these words in Austin, the capital of Texas:

> The march continued at a steady pace until we arrived at the corner of Congress and Sixth Street. Congress and Sixth Street are where the bars are, where the partying goes on and a lot of immorality and wickedness — it's a real stronghold of our city.
>
> When the group of pastors reached that intersection the procession stopped. I don't know what the reason was, but the police stopped, the procession stopped, everything stopped — so the pastors were stranded right there in the intersection of Sixth Street and Congress. Just at that moment the praise march moved into the song "Lord, Have Mercy on This Nation." The Spirit of God came and moved in the hearts of the pastors with real repentance, and they all fell on their knees and cried out to God for His mercy, especially for that very important part of our city.

As soon as that song was over, the procession began to move again and proceeded up Congress Avenue to the south steps of the capitol building where we gathered. As the pastors joined hands, the Spirit of God joined hearts.

Like Jesus, in fact *with* Jesus, we need to identify with the city, not distance ourselves from it prudishly or delight in its downfall. As we do so, let us remind ourselves that the price of Jesus' identification with the people was much more than tears wept over them. Not only had He lived His life for them, but He was about to lay down His life for them. If we choose to join Jesus as He weeps over a city, we may find that we will also share in His rejection. Yet the tragedy of the cross was turned into tremendous joy as crucifixion was followed by resurrection, ascension by Pentecost and Pentecost by the gathering in of thousands of new believers.

When Jesus offered Himself as a sacrifice for our sins, it was the ultimate intercession. Jesus did more than speak prayers. Every fiber of His being *was* prayer, as Gethsemane and Golgotha illustrate so poignantly. Although we may speak or sing words of prayer during a march, what we are doing *is* an act of prayer in a very real sense. In the same way genuine faith can be expressed by spoken prayers, faith can be expressed by our actions and our bodies. This became very real to me during long-distance prayer walks. We would pray aloud most of the day in groups of two or three, but there were times when we knew that the very action of walking through the land was a prayer of faith.

I suppose Jesus could have wept over Jerusalem from inside a synagogue or in Lazarus's lounge at Bethany. Perhaps there were times when He did, but his deepest identification with the city took place on location with the city spread out before Him. Similarly our identification with and intercession for the city becomes especially real and urgent when the subject of our prayers is also the object in our vision. Rather than depending upon our imaginations, our five senses are full of information. We see real people; we pass the centers of power or the locations of special need. We interact with our environment, instead of with our scant impressions of it.

EIGHT

PROCLAIMING TRUTH

The crowd that accompanied Jesus into Jerusalem may have misunderstood the nature of the kingdom they were proclaiming. Though their allegiance wavered when the shadow of arrest and trial fell over their hero, they proclaimed truth. In the same way, after Peter confessed that Jesus was Christ, he made a comment that earned Jesus' stern rebuke of "Get behind Me, Satan" (see Mark 8:29-33). Peter's misstatement did not invalidate the truth he had just spoken. Therefore, Jesus received the acclamations of the crowd and resisted those who tried to make Him silence them. Whatever else might have been lacking, they had taken hold of truth, Scripture verses packed with prophetic significance, and that has a power all of its own.

All the marches that I have had the privilege of being involved with have centered around the bold and joyful proclamation of truth about Jesus. This has been done largely in songs, shouts or corporate readings of Scripture verses. A musical idea which came during the writing of the music for the first *Make Way* march album developed into a song based upon the Apostles' Creed. This was as surprising to me as to anybody else because I did not have a liturgical background, yet it seemed entirely appropriate to the streets. As it was used I received comments concerning the sense of God's power that was released in this creedal proclamation. Was this just the sense of solidarity enjoyed as believers united with one voice to affirm the faith they shared? Or does the power of God come when the truth of God is proclaimed corporately with faith and authority? The first published march began with a responsive shout: "Make way for the King of kings." Does the kingdom of God make any inroads on the back of such an announcement?

A Proclamation Through the Powers

The very act of proclaiming truth in our public praise and worship is not only a proclamation in the presence of people but also a proclamation in the presence of spiritual powers. In other words, it is not so much a proclamation *to* the powers as it is a proclamation *through* them. To make sense of what I'm saying, let's look at the graphic language used by Paul to describe Christ's exaltation: "He raised Him from the dead, and seated Him at His right hand in the heavenly places, far above all rule and authority and power and dominion, and every name that is named" (Eph. 1:20-21).

Elsewhere Jesus is described as having "passed through the heavens" to that highest place of all (Heb. 4:14). In Ephesians 4:8 Paul quotes from Psalm 68:18: "When He ascended on high, He led captive a host of captives." In verse 10 he continued, "He who descended is Himself also He who ascended far above all the heavens, that He might fill all things."

The picture is clear. From His descent into death and Hades, Jesus rose and ascended through the heavens passing every rank of earthly and heavenly power until He reached the highest throne where He sat down to reign. Therefore because we have access to that glorious throne, we can offer worship through that corridor that Jesus opened for us, worship that itself is a demonstration of His glorious wisdom to the powers which He disarmed through the cross.

A Demonstration to the Powers

> To me, the very least of all saints, this grace was given, to preach to the Gentiles the unfathomable riches of Christ, and to bring to light what is the administration of the mystery which for ages has been hidden in God, who created all things; in order that the manifold wisdom of God might now be made known through the church to the rulers and the authorities in the heavenly places (Eph. 3:8-10).

A mystery from ages past is being brought to light; the multifaceted wisdom of God is being made known. But this is not only to the world of mankind. It is a demonstration to the powers in "heavenly places." These are the rulers and the authorities of the kind also referred to in Ephesians 1:21 and 6:12 and Colossians 2:10,15.

If you doubt that God wants to make His manifold wisdom known before the powers of heaven and hell, then you can also reread the story of Job.

The angelic powers are not described in Ephesians 3 as listening to what the saints may actually say. It simply reads that something will become known through the church. We may have more to say by demonstration than by declaration.

The praise march stands as a vast visual aid for God's people to help them grasp the free access to God opened for us in Christ. We cannot fully know all that takes place in the heavenlies as we worship, but this much must be clear to every angelic power: that Christ is victor over powers that have held His beloved people and that they now come to Him as loving children, willingly, in spirit and in truth and forever. No power in heaven can restrain them from free and fruitful intimacy with the One who sits on the throne.

In processional praise we act out the defeat of the powers. No wonder the passage which describes the church making something known to the heavenlies (Eph. 3:10) goes on without pause that such a manifestation to the powers is in accordance with God's eternal purpose, accomplished now in Christ. That purpose is immediately summed up in verse 12: "In whom we have boldness and confident access through faith in Him." The "access" is far more than slipping into heaven at the moment of death. Paul is still revelling in the glory of all of God's people, Jew and Gentile together, enjoying a present "access in one Spirit to the Father" (Eph. 2:13-18).

We cannot be absolutely certain about what makes an impression on such powers or what impression we need to make. But let these powers read our "body language." As we approach God as "one new man" as "one body to God," the coming glory of humanity will become clear (Eph. 2:15-16). Perhaps it might be more effective to tell heavenly powers to "Read my hips!" as we use the access to God's throne by walking down the street together.

Truth v. Lies

The devil's first foothold in humanity was achieved by tempting Eve to question God's words. The insidious and subtle strategy was couched in the words, "Did God really say?" After introducing doubt, Satan followed with a straight contradiction, then twisted and misapplied God's Word. Jesus described Satan's nature: "He was a murderer from the beginning, not holding to the truth, for there is no truth in him. When he lies, he speaks his native language, for he is a liar and the father of lies" (John 8:44, NIV). Lies, deception and half-truths are the devil's native language. He has used them to blind the nations and take them captive through the ages. Jesus said, "You will know the truth, and the truth will set you free" (John 8:32, NIV). If everybody in the world knew and obeyed the truth about God and salvation through Jesus, they would immediately be set free from Satan's power. However the sad scenario is this: "The god of this age has blinded the minds of unbelievers, so that they cannot see the light of the gospel of the glory of Christ" (2 Cor. 4:4, NIV).

Truth and the spiritual light that streams from it are a devastating weapon against the devil and his kingdom. This is well expressed by Roger Forster and Paul Marston:

> Words of truth are like light, in that both reveal an object or person for what it or he is. Those whose deeds are evil are afraid to come into the light. Through the weapons of truth and light Christ will finally reveal evil for what it is, and in doing so will destroy it. In the full revelation of what it is, evil shrivels up and is destroyed.[1]

How will Satan finally be destroyed? Paul informs us: "And then shall that wicked be revealed, whom the Lord shall consume with the spirit of his mouth, and shall destroy with the brightness of his coming" (2 Thess. 2:8, KJV). Satan will be consumed by spirit-energized words of truth from the lips of Jesus and destroyed as surely as light annihilates darkness.

Let us be reminded that the weapons with which we do battle in the spiritual realm and the armor that protects us are not our weapons or armor, but Christ's. The sword in our hand is not the sword of the believer, but the sword of the Spirit which is the Word of God. We are told to put on the "whole armor of God" (Eph. 6:11, KJV).

In our victory procession we are not an irresistible force striking an immovable object. We are an irresistible force (Christ in us, all His power and authority at the Father's right hand), striking what is, in contrast to the power of the cross, a flimsy fabrication of lies, deception, half-truths and spent power. A piece of paper folded a number of times and stood on its end will bear some weight. When it is straightened out it can support nothing at all. Similarly when we straighten out the crookedness of Satan's lies by declaring the truth about God, his devices are robbed of their strength and his stratagems crumble.

The Power of Words

Every day countless billions of words spoken in the world mold lives and circumstances for good or for evil. The deepest hurts we receive nearly always come from words. A broken bone will heal, and the place will be stronger than before. A broken heart never mends in that way apart from the love of God.

Words release more than mere information — they

release spiritual energy. Jesus said the food that goes into a man's mouth does not defile him, but rather the words that come out of his mouth. The true nature of a person cannot be detached from their words. "For out of the overflow of the heart the mouth speaks. The good man brings good things out of the good stored up in him, and the evil man brings evil things out of the evil stored up in him" (Matt. 12:34-35, NIV). Human beings were created with a spiritual dimension. Jesus explained that the spirit of a person reaches out through their words to bless or to curse, to spread a fragrance of holiness or the stench of sin.

We are also familiar with the way music expresses the spirit of the composer, singer or instrumentalist in a way that can be felt in the spirit of the listener. Words and music together are a powerful thing. While words that we speak or sing can have a positive effect in the spiritual dimension, many times others will use words for evil. Words can release the spiritual energy of Satan and his fallen angels when people make room for evil in their lives. In the same way, people who are seeking the Spirit of God can find it in the Scripture verses, songs and shouts of the praise marches.

However, the most powerful words in the whole existence are the words of God. Through spoken word God created the world and called into being things that did not previously exist. God the Son spoke, and blind eyes were opened, the lame walked, and even the dead were raised. The molecules and cells of human bodies were recreated or reshaped by His words of faith.

On one occasion an unfruitful fig tree was cursed, and it withered shortly afterward. On another occasion a storm at sea was stilled in a moment. Jesus described His words in this way, "The words that I have spoken to you are spirit and are life" (John 6:63). Because God Himself was the source of Jesus' words, they were truth in themselves. They were also endorsed as truth by the accompanying activity of the Holy Spirit. As Jesus preached the good news of the kingdom of God, signs and wonders followed. His words were not just sound waves carried across the air. They were the very breath of God, creating or destroying by the power of the Holy Spirit.

One of the weapons of the "overcomers" in the final scenes of the book of Revelation will be sacrifice: the sacrifice of Christ, the Lamb of God, and the sacrifice of their own lives. The other weapon will be "the word of their testimony" (Rev. 12:11). We can never underestimate the power of God's truth spoken in faith out of personal experience. We do not realize the immensity of this weapon, so let us remind ourselves that the final battle with Satan is at least fifty percent won with Holy Spirit-energized words!

Prophetic Symbolism

This is possibly an unfamiliar term for many Christians and yet the Bible is packed with prophetic symbolism: Moses lifting his rod over the Red Sea or holding his hands in prayer over the battleground with Aaron and Hur on either side, Joshua walking seven times around Jericho, Jesus writing in the sand and so on.

Such prophetic actions seem to be a trigger point for the power of God to be released, so I believe it would be a mistake to consign such prophetic symbolism to the pages of the Bible. In fact, we use symbols thousands of times a day right now. Whenever we speak, we are using symbols because words in themselves are just vibrations through the air. They have meaning because we associate the vocabulary of sounds with objects around us and feelings inside us. We all have an assumption that words can release spiritual power. We believe when we preach the gospel that the Holy Spirit can take the sound symbols of our words and ride upon them in power into people's lives. So why not actions as well?

There is a powerful symbolism in public praise events — a great mass of people standing together, moving as one, perhaps joining hands, uniting in creedal statements, carrying banners which are themselves symbols, marching in step, cooperating together. But it is not just symbol. It is substance. That substance is the faith which is being exercised by the multiplied participants as they "put their foot down" in the Lord's name. Time and time again the Scriptures tell of men, women and children of God who, in obedience to God, did apparently futile or foolish things. They acted in faith and inflicted great damage on the kingdom of darkness.

Jean Darnall tells a fascinating story about a visit to Australia. She was among a group of Christians who felt they should pray concerning a red-light district where prostitution was rampant. The breakthrough came when she felt stirred to do something which might have seemed rather strange. Standing on a chair underneath a lamppost, she began simply to sing God's praises. Shortly afterward, for no apparent reason, prostitutes with packed suitcases were seen leaving the buildings.

Perhaps you could argue that the effect might have been the same if she had sat in a comfortable church lounge and prayed. Yet I wonder whether there was an important significance in being in the actual place where the prayers were being aimed.

In several cities in Great Britain church leaders have set out to encircle their cities in marches. It's an expression of their belief that "the earth is the Lord's and everything in it" — including the city. Birmingham, Britain's second largest city, was encircled in one day by ten different marches, starting from ten different places. They marched simultaneously, covering almost thirty miles of boundary in not much more than an hour and a half. Edinburgh has been systematically encircled section by section over a period of time as a deliberate symbolic act of surrounding the city and proclaiming that Christ is King and Lord over it.

The symbol and celebration without the daily application will, of course, become worse than empty. But great joy and encouragement, as well as testimony, are in the symbol. Catch most people mid-march and ask them why they are marching. Most answers will be summed up in the words "for Jesus."

NINE

THE HIGHEST COMMON DENOMINATOR

And those who went before, and those who followed after, were crying out, "Hosanna!" (Mark 11:9).

The Palm Sunday procession does not appear to qualify as a model of Christian unity. It was a brief and spontaneous affair. Whatever cohesiveness it generated seemed to have evaporated by the end of that week. Though the participants were, for those few glorious moments, united in purpose and in praise, it could easily be written off as superficial, emotional and short-lived. But we are left with the problem that Zechariah prophesied it, and Jesus planned it, participated in it, received the praise, endorsed the content and refused to silence it. I invite you to put aside preconceived ideas and see here a brief, but exhilarating, glimpse of something powerful concerning the nature of Jesus' kingdom.

A more disparate group could hardly be imagined. At the core were the twelve, and their diversity, rivalry and social incompatibility are well known. There were other disciples, very likely including the women who are reported to have travelled with Him ministering to His needs. Beggars from the gates of Jericho, freshly healed and jubilant, followed Him with many other brand-new believers, as yet undiscipled and untaught (see Luke 18:35-19:28). There were sincere seekers and curiosity seekers, witnesses of the miracles and voyeurs of the miraculous (see John 12:9).

Mixed in with these may have been some with political ambitions, shouting children and starchy religious experts. Some had come all the way with Him, and some just came out of the city to meet Him, elements both of costly discipleship and superficial pop religion. There were feast-goers from the Jewish nation and from many distant nations (John 12:20). The Pharisees summed it up when they muttered despairingly to one another, "You see that you are not doing any good; look, the world has gone after Him" (John 12:19)

This disparate crowd, their attention magnetized to Jesus, had suddenly, if briefly, become one, chanting the same Scripture verses, singing the same psalm. Matthew and Mark both report that the multitudes going before Him and those following after Him took up the same acclamations. Luke reports that the whole multitude of the disciples began to praise God joyfully with a loud voice. Those who escorted Him down the Mount of Olives and those who ran out to meet Him from Jerusalem were unanimous in their choice of shouts and palm-waving welcome. The only dissident voices reported are those who would not praise Him. Humanly speaking, the potential for disintegration and confusion was vast, but Jesus was not intimidated. Under His leadership, what could have been a mob became a glorious procession.

The key to it all was the focus upon Jesus. His twelve trusted friends that gathered around Him formed a solid core of prophetic praise. Around them the other groups spread out like concentric circles in diminishing degrees of allegiance or familiarity with Him, yet magnetized to the one center, united in focus, vocalizing the same truth. This may not be a model for normal church worship, but it could be a model for certain times when God calls the church to parade Jesus before the world. The story of a march in Toronto, Canada, demonstrates how an unexpected combination of people can unite together in praise to the King. A core of about twenty believers from the Church of St. George the Martyr led more than three hundred non-Christians in a praise and prayer march and miraculously got their full participation.

There is a dimension here that I believe may manifest itself more and more as the church goes public, something that flows out of the unified core of those who love Jesus. This synthesis of human beings does not create unity of the organizational, institutional or structural kind. Instead it causes a radical reorientation of a whole city, turning all eyes to Jesus. Palm Sunday was not a moment of mass conversion, though many were on the journey to becoming disciples. It was a moment of revelation, a moment of visitation.

> And the glory which Thou hast given Me I have given to them; that they may be one, just as We are one; I in them, and Thou in Me, that they may be perfected in unity, that the world may know that Thou didst send Me, and didst love them, even as Thou didst love Me (John 17:22-23).

When I wrote the music for the first *Make Way* march album, I imagined that perhaps a few of the radical fellowships might take it up; but I was not so sure about the more conservative churches. Yet as reports flowed into the mailbox, the most dominant feature was that churches were coming together on the streets around Jesus. The process of organizing the march had been a catalyst for a new spirit of cooperation among the churches. Much more than that, however, there seemed to be a groundswell of desire to stand together in the name of Jesus and to go public in His name arm-in-arm rather than independently. Sometimes attempts at Christian unity gravitate toward the lowest common denominator and the result is negotiations around divisive issues of doctrine or practice. But the worship motive causes us to ascend to the level of the highest common denominator, as all eyes are lifted in admiration of the One who has captured all our hearts. Churches uniting in this way give a powerful contradiction to a world which is convinced that the church is hopelessly divided. Much more than that, as we turn our eyes to Jesus, they look to see where we are looking — and see Him.

So praise marches have become events in which, as they have rallied to Jesus, Christians have discovered one another and enjoyed sharing the common ground beginning with Him. From this starting point they discover that the rest of the common ground is far bigger than they first thought. Furthermore, marches are a visual aid for how God brings people together. It is profound when people of different races, cultures, classes, generations, traditions, denominations and conditions move as one, sing the same songs, pray the same prayers and unite in the same Spirit.

In a paper explaining March for Jesus in the United Kingdom Roger Forster wrote:

> When Jesus prayed "that they may all be one...that the world may believe" (John 17:21), He did not expect to wait two thousand years for it to happen. It is an insult to the

Father (and it would certainly put me off my prayer life) if Jesus had to wait two thousand years for an answer to prayer. Within hours of the prayer, "I pray that they may be one," Jesus went to the cross and was crucified so that every difference and distinction, everything that is a barrier in our relationships, everything that stands in the way of the human race being reconciled, might be nailed to the cross. Then He rose as one new man, carrying with Him a totally new humanity that could never be anything but wholly at one with each other. If we are not one with each other it is because we will not receive the unity of the Spirit which is the gift of God which Paul enjoins us to keep, not make (Eph. 4:1-3).

We do not gather on the streets to generate unity but to celebrate it! What a waste of time it would be to attempt to create something that has already been given to us freely and at such a price. The realization of unity is severely hindered, however, if we confuse unity with uniformity. They are not the same. Wherever Jesus' disciples are described, uniformity is markedly absent!

Ray Mayhew, a fellow leader at the Ichthus Christian Fellowship, points out that Parthians, Medes, Egyptians, Libyans and Arabs were baptized together on the day of Pentecost, regardless of nationality (see Acts 2:9-11). Later, a Cypriot, a black African, an Arab and a Jew worked together as a leadership team (see Acts 13:1-2). The nucleus of the emerging church at Philippi is formed by the unlikely combination of a wealthy Asian business-woman, a Greek slave and a Roman civil servant (see Acts 16). What a testimony this is to a world forever disintegrating because of such differences.

Because our eyes are fixed upon Jesus, amazed by His capacity to receive those whom we would disqualify, we gain faith to receive one another. Instead of being threatened by diversity, we learn to celebrate it and embrace our differences. By valuing diversity, we release others from the burden of our expectations of them, encouraging each diverse group to bring its unique contribution.

There is an element of risk here, especially where a wide diversity of doctrine is represented in the groups at the core of the event. But the best safeguard to orthodoxy is the same one which enabled Jesus' procession to proclaim the same truths with one voice. They united around a common creed, prophetically pertinent to the occasion. In their case the creed was taken from Psalm 118, a central part of the liturgy of the feast which they were celebrating at the time. At the heart of our marches and public praise events have been carefully prepared scripts built around the central truths of the Christian faith, expressed through Scripture verses, songs, shouts and sometimes actual creeds, notably the Apostles' Creed.

It is impossible to please everybody and every group all the time. However, believers of diverse traditions and backgrounds have overwhelmingly united on this glorious common ground of truth. It has also created a natural safeguard against extreme groups or cults participating. The printed program is available in advance and those who cannot assent to the content tend to opt out ahead of time.

A substantial part of the program has been the recorded praise march music, containing songs which express the core truths and the prophetic thrust of the marches. Songs like "Shine, Jesus, Shine" have helped to sum up a widely felt desire for nationwide revival. Where such songs become widely known, they offer more common ground around which to unite on the streets.

Coming together in a spirit of unity is itself a powerful act of spiritual warfare. It declares to the powers of darkness that they are disarmed and doomed because in Christ we are reconciled and brought together in love at the foot of the cross. In the presence of heaven and earth we give testimony to Jesus, in whom "all things hold together," and to the wisdom of the Father's plan "through Him to reconcile all things to Himself, having made peace through the blood of His cross" (Col. 1:17,20).

Paul in writing to the Ephesians spoke of the manifold wisdom of God being made known through the church to the rulers and authorities in the heavenly places (see Eph. 3:10). This verse is set in the context of reconciliation between Jew and Gentile, extreme groups finding in the cross of Christ common access to the Father. To heaven and earth an authentic demonstration of such reconciliation is almost unbelievable. The explanation is Christ, and the glory flows to Him.

The gospel is going to be preached to the ends of the earth. The task must be complete within one generation, or the next one grows up, and the job has to begin over again. But it will not be done unless we do it together. Cities will not be taken for Christ until the churches bury their differences and do it together. Churches working together in this way produce greater results than cooperation, pooling of resources and so on. Buried beneath centuries of backbiting, infighting, jealousy and insecurity lies a spiritual weapon of devastating power. It is a sword of such enormity that it cannot be picked up and used by a single pair of hands. It is the equipment of a great warrior, but the warrior is corporate not individual. The warrior is the worldwide body of Christ, and the weapon is "that they may be one...that the world may know that Thou didst send Me" (John 17:22-23).

Breaking Walls of Division

Satan's power is vested in division. His initial power base came because he succeeded in dividing creature from Creator through sin. Within a generation, motivated by jealousy, brother had murdered brother. Before long, nation was slaughtering nation. In the crucifixion of Jesus every dividing wall of hostility was broken down. It remains for us to step over the rubble, embrace one another and celebrate what He has achieved. The devil's great fear is that Christians across the world will have their eyes opened to see that the walls are down, that we are already one in Christ.

Interestingly, of all the songs in the book of Revelation, not one is a solo. The twenty-four elders sing and cast their crowns before His feet, the united voices of countless angels resound, every living creature in heaven and earth and under the earth and all that is in them are joined in one song. Those who are victorious over the beast are given harps and a song to sing, the "song of Moses the servant of God and the song of the Lamb" (Rev. 15:3, NIV). In every case multitudes of peoples or angels unite in the same song with absolute unity, with one voice.

The same is true of many of the shouts of Revelation. Though there are countless voices, not one is dissenting. "Then I heard what sounded like a great multitude, like the roar of rushing waters and like loud peals of thunder, shouting: 'Hallelujah! For our Lord God Almighty reigns. Let us rejoice and be glad and give him glory!' " (Rev. 19:6-7, NIV). Most of us know the excitement of hearing twenty thousand voices roar together as a goal is scored at a football match. Or we know the sense of awe which is created by hearing a massed choir of thousands singing praise to God. But how can we imagine the sound of innumerable men and angels singing with one voice under the arches of heaven? It will be indescribable.

Though we can't imagine the sounds of heaven, we can begin here on earth to offer worship in cooperation with other believers because God is building believers together into a spiritual house of worship (see 1 Pet. 2:5). We do not wait for heaven. We take hold of heaven's kingdom now and bring it into the earth. We do not sit waiting for perfected Christians to show up with whom to be united. Rather we seek those whose eyes are also fixed adoringly upon Jesus, and we agree to march together in celebration that in Him every dividing wall has been broken down. And as we do, we find ourselves moving like an army, shoulder to shoulder, our feet and hearts in step with one another and with heaven's battalions.

If we are to be consistent within the context of a public praise event, the principle and practice of unity has to work upward and outward from the leadership roots of the event to the furthest tips of the rank and file branches. Vested interests have to be laid down, competitiveness surrendered, fears and insecurities confessed, personality promotion and power plays banished. The pathway to the goodness and pleasantness of dwelling together in unity is bound to be costly. But if it leads to a place where through the perfecting of unity the world sees Jesus revealed, then it is a price well worth paying with a glad heart.

TEN

PREPARING FOR THE HARVEST

And they were on the road, going up to Jerusalem, and Jesus was walking on ahead of them; and they were amazed, and those who followed were fearful (Mark 10:32).

The disciples were following a determined Jesus. He had resolutely set His face to go to Jerusalem where He would complete all that the Father had asked Him to do. His face was set like a flint as He walked on ahead of them toward Jericho, the last city before the capital. Predictably those who followed Him were fearful. It was no comfort when He took the twelve aside and informed them that betrayal, arrest, scourging and crucifixion awaited Him there. I wonder how many quietly dropped out of His entourage around that time, questioning the sanity of continuing the journey. But though fearful, to their credit, it seems that many continued with Him long enough to see their fear banished.

This nervous group on the way to Jericho was quite a contrast to the triumphant crowd they became shortly afterward. In fact, the greatest outbreak of praise came when they finally faced that which had come to symbolize their fears, the city of Jerusalem. Jesus climbed on a donkey fetched from a nearby village, and the crowd became a procession. The source of their fears was before them, but so was Jesus. All at once they exalted their King and forgot their fears. The murmurs of anxiety were replaced by cries of "hosanna" and "Blessed is He who comes in the name of the Lord."

We too are following a determined Jesus. He is determined to bring His purposes on earth to a glorious consummation and looks to us to share in them. The apostle John reports, "He who testifies to these things says, 'Yes, I am coming quickly.' " And we reply, "Amen. Come, Lord Jesus" (Rev. 22:20). Yet, like the disciples, we often lag behind as Jesus strides ahead, discussing our anxieties and enumerating what might go wrong. Up to this point, the disciples had paid a modest price to follow Jesus. But as confrontation with the authorities loomed ominously close, the stakes suddenly leapt frighteningly high. We love the concept and prospect of Christ's kingdom coming upon the earth, but we are not always so sure about the implications of removing the present kingdoms of the world.

We need a baptism of boldness. We need to come face-to-face with what we fear, shouting hosannas, combining our petition and our praise. One of the first things I observed about praise marches was this transformation of a nervous, anxious crowd into a bold, joyful procession. As people assemble and prepare to march, especially for the first time, many fears are being faced — fears of the unknown, uncertainties about what to do, how to behave. Will there be opposition? Will I look foolish? Will I be recognized and have to explain myself later to incredulous or cynical friends, coworkers or neighbors? Leaders may fear the event will flop, and they will lose credibility with those who followed them.

The Foolishness of Marching

It is not surprising to find that much of the resistance to the concept of public praise arises from the embarrassment potential of such overt demonstrations of commitment. Here many of us discover how free we truly are or how much we fear censure by others.

One of the unwritten rules of my own social training was: Don't make a fuss, especially in public places. Causing heads to turn or inviting unwelcome attention was to break the code of conformity. Blending into the background was the skill to be applauded. One of my first public appearances in a musical context was as a guitarist in an evangelistic band. I was so terrified that my fingers more or less refused to cooperate with my brain. I was paralyzed by an audience — about eight people at that time.

All of us are subject to peer pressure, which is really a euphemism for what the Scriptures call "the fear of man." On one level it is not unreasonable to be sympathetic to one another's fears of censure. After all, outside of a revelation of God the Father's unconditional love, we are all to some degree hostage to the opinions of our peers. We determine our self-esteem by how much we have been loved or despised.

But in the revelation of God's love comes a liberation from a power that is nothing less than slavery: "For you have not received a spirit of slavery leading to fear again, but you have received a spirit of adoption as sons by which we cry out, 'Abba! Father!' " (Rom. 8:15). The spirit of slavery causes us to implode in morbid introspection and repressed anger, but the spirit of adoption brings an explosion of uninhibited joy. The spirit of adoption announces to the world the death of the old slavemaster and the resurrection reign of the One who rules by love and adopts the spiritually orphaned. In one sense, public praise is a corporate orchestration of that spirit-energized cry, a celebration of sonship on a grand scale.

Some people's consciences or convictions may inhibit them from public expressions of praise. Others wisely seek for the divine mandate on timing or question the methodology in a particular culture or context. Without question, these are concerns we should respect. However, I suspect that the objections from some quarters arise from less noble considerations. They may be an attempt to justify a predisposition to remain within the comfort zones offered by conformity to the prevailing social or religious norms.

In fact, street demonstrations of one kind or another are a feature of most societies and cultures, from Mayday military parades to carol singing, from the Chinese new year celebrations to revolutionary uprisings, from Mardi Gras to militant gay parades. The method is universally familiar and its validity generally assumed. It is the reason for the demonstration that determines how costly participation is because different causes invite differing degrees of approval or censure.

Fear of censure is surely one of the most potent forces by which the powers of darkness keep the church contained within its buildings. We can become so used to living whole lifetimes in the rarefied atmospheres of religious buildings and Christian activities that the potential for conflict with the world is sometimes out of the realm of possibility. I find it revealing to observe the signs of agitation in a crowd that is assembling to march for the first time. I know the fears that are surfacing as they anticipate going public for perhaps the first time. Yet I smile because I know that within a very short time the same people are going to go through a transformation. About halfway down the route, their confession of Christ as Lord will gather momentum, and a "spell" will be broken. This is the "spell of silence" that settles subtly upon the church when public testimony to Jesus Christ falls into neglect.

The Spell of Silence

My reading of the Scriptures leads me to believe that this spell of silence is more than mere absence of vocal and physical testimony to Christ. The lack of confession of Christ is a passive submission to the actual spiritual power of the prince of the power of the air.

Describing the kind of saints who finally overcome the devil, the "loud voice in heaven" of the book of Revelation says, "They overcame him because of the blood of the Lamb and because of the word of their testimony, and they did not love their life even to death" (Rev. 12:9,11). There is power in the blood, as saints have sung for centuries, but the power is released only as we testify to it. And a testimony is not a testimony until it is expressed — a witness can be called to the witness box and still fail to speak out what he knows and believes to be the truth for fear of the consequences.

The streets have increasingly become the "witness box" of the world observed by millions through the remote eyes and ears of TV cameras, radios and tape recorders. I believe that God is calling His witness, the church, into the global witness box to testify to the truth of the power of the gospel of Jesus Christ. The church will heap up evidence to condemn the god of this world, Satan, and expose his counterfeit kingdom for what it is.

If we love our own lives more than we love our Lord Jesus Christ, our testimony will be muted the moment the stakes are raised. I have to be honest and admit that most of my objections to public acknowledgment of Christ are rooted in my self-love. I do not wish to appear foolish or fanatical. I do not wish to be associated with those who might appear foolish or fanatical. I do not want to appear "uncool." I am nervous about the risk of criticism if I march with groups that other groups disapprove of. And what if there is a counter demonstration with the risk of verbal or physical abuse? Now in my experience these fears rarely materialize, but I know their source — I love my own life!

Except for the minority of gung ho enthusiasts, most of us can identify with fear. Few of us realize, however, that when we touch these areas we are touching the pressure points which the powers of darkness use to rule over us. Jesus became flesh and blood so that "through death He might render powerless him who had the power of death, that is, the devil; and might deliver those who through fear of death were subject to slavery all their lives" (Heb. 2:14-15). How much is the church still in slavery because of fear of death to our reputations, our respectability or our comfort?

The most dangerous criminal is the one with nothing left to lose, with a death sentence already passed and a catalogue of crimes already committed. Similarly the saint most dangerous to the kingdom of darkness is the one who has received the death sentence to his own desires, whether those desires are legitimate or otherwise. That one has nothing left to lose because he already gave it all away to the One he loves. The prayers and deeds of such a person carry great power and authority.

Denying Self

In a crucifixion the arms, the most basic means of self-defense, are outstretched, exposing the body and denying all means of protection. Refusing to surrender to the natural instinct to save Himself, Jesus gave His hands — the hands that flung stars into space — to the crucifiers. He became "obedient to the point of death, even death on a cross" (Phil. 2:8).

This very act of self-giving sent shock waves of horror through the strongholds of hell as it delivered the fatal blow to him who rules by the fear of death. To those who witnessed the crucifixion — the traumatized and grief-stricken disciples, the mocking Pharisees, the indifferent soldiers, the powers of heaven and hell — it must have seemed that death had triumphed. But it was not as it seemed. The perfect, sinless Son of God had died, but in His death grip He held tightly to the powers of death, disease, decay and destruction. He took them into His death, breaking their power and disarming them!

The story is told of a Christian suffering intense physical torture because of his refusal to deny his Savior. As the torturer threatened the believer with death, the Christian responded, "To kill me is your greatest weapon. To die is mine."

Every act of dying to self, from the little ones we face daily and hourly, to the ultimate one, is an act of war. They are sure and certain invasions of territories that would otherwise be the unchallenged domain of the god of this world. If going public is sometimes costly, then the higher the price tag, the greater the victory will be.

That is why public confession of Christ has a value that goes beyond merely advancing the kingdom of heaven on earth. It resonates to the very heart of our relationship with Jesus and to the very core of our being. Peter knew what confession meant when the searching eyes of the Master, whom he had so recently denied, looked deep into his soul, and Jesus asked, "Simon, son of John, do you love Me?" (John 21:17). To love Jesus is not to be ashamed of Him. If He publicly suffers shame, He calls us to share in it with Him. It is not a question of duty but of devotion.

As the other disciples stood by, I am convinced the same question pierced their own souls. They were mindful of the fact that though Peter had failed the test, they had avoided it by going into hiding! Perhaps the previous words of Jesus flooded back, "For whoever is ashamed of Me and My words in this adulterous and sinful generation, the Son of Man will also be ashamed of him when He comes in the glory of His Father with the holy angels" (Mark 8:38).

The Status Quo

The status quo of the powers of Peter's day — the Pharisees, the Romans and the mob — had determined that Jesus was no longer to be tolerated, and allegiance to Him was no longer permissible. The time is right to challenge by demonstration the power of public opinion that 1) considers Christianity should be practiced behind closed doors, 2) is being persuaded that no efforts should be made to evangelize people of other faiths or no faith at all, and 3) avoids the name of Jesus except as an expletive. The time is right in the West to break the shame we have allowed to come upon us because of our silence and to let our love for Jesus overflow in rivers of joy down our streets, no matter what the status quo of society dictates.

After all, failure to speak out is usually acquiescence to the status quo. Those of us in the "free" West may be especially guilty. Even though the price of public allegiance to Christ is still reasonably inexpensive, we often prefer not to pay it. If we will not pay when it is cheap, what will we do when it is expensive?

Every believer who has ever spoken out for Jesus in

front of family, friends or strangers knows that alongside the fears and the sense of vulnerability come an inner strength and fresh courage. Though there is safety in numbers in corporate public praise, I have observed time and time again a baptism of boldness coming upon the believers as they speak out in mass acts of testimony to their street, town, city or even nation.

A Climate for Evangelism

> And when He had entered Jerusalem, all the city was stirred, saying, "Who is this?" (Matt. 21:10).

So the noisy cavalcade reaches the ancient walls, and "all the city is stirred." Now the urban infrastructure amplifies the hosannas and noise of general commotion, swelling the crowds with onlookers. From joy to indignation, from curiosity to amusement, from surprise to wonder, from hope to anger, the population must have provided a whole gamut of reactions. The cry goes up, "Who is this?" The answer is passed rapidly through the crowds, up and down the dusty streets, shouted through doorways and up to rooftops: "This is the prophet Jesus, from Nazareth in Galilee" (Matt. 21:11).

Is it not time that the people of God stirred whole cities? Is it not overdue that the church ceased trying to blend into the general background, scared to upset the status quo? But stirring a city in itself may not always be a good thing. Cities can be stirred by scandals or by ecclesiastical folly on a grand scale or by clever and expensive promotional campaigns. The question we want on the lips of a city population is not, What was that? but, Who is this?

While the church is busy answering questions that

nobody is asking, she has forgotten how to be an event which demands an explanation. The event desired is not a crusade or a program or even a march, though these may be useful frameworks. The event is a Person, a Person who demands an introduction. On that day when Jesus rode into Jerusalem, the spiritual climate of the city was radically affected. From going about their normal business of life, everyone stopped to ask the most crucial question of all. It is a question we want on the lips of every person on the face of the earth, and we want to be ready to answer it.

A praise march is not essentially an evangelistic method. If such a method is being sought, there are many to choose from. But its effect in the end may be to prepare the way for great harvests of souls to be reaped. The key to its success in this respect is the preservation of its purity as a bold and extravagant display of love for Jesus, a joyful and confident celebration of the truth about Him. As such it can create a climate for evangelism.

The first and obvious way this works is that the phenomenon of hundreds or thousands of people in festive procession needs an explanation. Curiosity has to be satisfied, and the disturbance of the status quo has to be rationalized.

Stirring the Unseen City

Marching brings a shift in the spiritual climate. When a city is stirred, it is inevitably a spiritual affair. Can you imagine the inhabitants of the spiritual world continuing to go about their daily business when all the people they are trying to keep in darkness have stopped theirs in order to push to the front of the crowd and take a long look at the Light of the world?

Cities are not exclusively the expression of the people

who build them and live in them. Whether consciously or not every human being is profoundly influenced by, and interacts with, the unseen spiritual world. Where people congregate, so do spiritual powers. Through the medium of social structures, from family to institutional government, they combine to form the ideas which in turn form the city.

Spiritual powers find their expression through human beings, through their ideologies, their laws, their culture and their religion. Therefore, when Jesus rode into Jerusalem and the whole city was stirred, surely the city of the unseen powers was simultaneously agog.

Although it falls to some degree into the realm of the subjective, many Christians are aware of a discernible spiritual atmosphere in their neighborhood or city. They are also aware of changes in it brought about by prayer and worship. Some places are more responsive than others to the preaching of the gospel. When the spiritual history is traced, evidence sometimes comes to light which suggests why. An interesting report came to my attention from a coastal resort in the south of England.

> We discovered that during the last century there had been a fisherman's church on the seafront which had been knocked down to make way for redevelopment and relocated slightly inland on the London Road. The fishermen had apparently been so angry that they put a curse on the church, on the vicar who made the decision to move, and on subsequent vicars. It's strange but we had actually sensed real opposition along this stretch of road, even though it was ideal for evangelism because it only had pedestrian traffic.
>
> Our praise march took us past this site,

although we hadn't chosen the route with that in mind. Each of the participating churches does evangelism in that area, and we noticed a clear difference in responses after the march by the following summer when we had a visiting evangelistic team working there. Forty people were saved on that stretch of road over a one-month period. Our local March for Jesus in 1991 followed the same route; only this time we had a crack evangelism team coming along behind doing street drama, preaching and personal work. Over the two hours following the march we saw nine people make first-time commitments to Jesus on that stretch of road.

There is much that we do not yet understand in the matter of localized encounters with spiritual powers. We also still need to learn what is actually going on when we have evidence of a change in the spiritual "atmosphere." In this respect I welcome the recent increase in theological debate. Meanwhile it is enough for praise marchers to know that in the act of giving glory to God, His kingdom has advanced in discernible ways. They rejoice because their names are written in heaven not because spiritual powers have been subjected to them.

ELEVEN

A HOUSE OF PRAYER FOR ALL NATIONS

And He began to teach and say to them, "Is it not written, 'My house shall be called a house of prayer for all the nations'?" (Mark 11:17).

Jesus culminated His praise march in the temple. Though it seemed a suitable end point, it was an even greater beginning.

As the hosannas of the children rang in the ears of the indignant chief priests and teachers of the law, they had strong reasons to demand that such words should be silenced. The children and the triumphant crowd before them were singing parts of the Hallel, phrases from Psalm 118. This was the reason for their discomfort because the psalm prophesied that the stone which the builders rejected would become the chief cornerstone. In other words, the Messiah who would be welcomed with cries of "hosanna" and "Blessed is He who comes in the name of the Lord" would not be recognized by the "builders," the official priesthood. Jesus was bringing to an end the era of the physical temple, judging it in its failure and corruption and inaugurating a new, spiritual temple, Himself the choice and precious cornerstone.

This prophetic act was finally sealed when Jesus gave up His Spirit on the cross, and the veil of the temple was torn supernaturally from top to bottom. It was a sign that now, through the "curtain" of the torn body of Jesus and through His shed blood, the way was open into the holy of holies, into the very presence of God. Had a particularly bold priest in Jerusalem risked a look through that torn curtain, he would have found nothing. The presence of God, the manifestation of His glory, had gone to dwell in another temple, one being built out of "living stones." A new city of Jerusalem had been founded, the one the apostle John described. "And I saw no temple in it, for the Lord God, the Almighty, and the Lamb, are its temple" (Rev. 21:22).

The destination of Jesus' march was the temple. The immeasurable significance of His goal only becomes clear in the light of the biblical story of the building of the house of God. The biblical record of God's dealings with mankind reveals a divine building program. The longing of God's heart is to dwell with His people, to enjoy the sweet fellowship of Eden so tragically broken by sin. God's early promise to make His dwelling among His people (Ex. 29:45-46) finds its utter fulfillment in the new city of God. "Behold, the tabernacle of God is among men, and He shall dwell among them, and they shall be His people, and God Himself shall be among them" (Rev. 21:3).

But throughout human history, as long as God has had a special people, He has offered to them an abundant, though partial, experience of His dwelling. He can be seen steadily unfolding the affairs of men, wooing hearts and defeating His enemies so that He can enjoy intimate habitation among His people.

The theme of the building of God's house is not a brief or shallow motif of Scripture. A list of some of the different physical structures that were built suggests distinct phases in God's building program. These phases are not a random scattering of punctuation marks in the epics of history. They are the very center point of the unfolding story.

What do buildings have to do with public praise? I've suggested that God is unwalling His people. Why muddle it all with ancient construction projects? The building of the house of God is of vast significance to those who step into public praise marching.

The significance is this: Every one of the major building projects of the house of God was preceded by a major procession. Just about every major procession culminates in the building of a house for God. The house of God is God's way to meet with His people. It is appropriate that a procession should characterize the process of establishing His presence and kingdom.

We will trace briefly the major phases of this building program. In relation to public praise marching, notice that every one of the houses of God was in some way a deeply satisfying fulfillment of the desires of God and His people. But each one also stirred hopes and desires for an even brighter fullness to come. So we can discern successively greater fulfillments, each stirring all hearts to a holy hunger for God's greater glory and dwelling on earth with His people. These events are not random episodes. Together they become a consistent story, into which we step today.

Watch as well for the theme of God bringing great fear and dread on His enemies that would withstand the procession of God.

1. The first building and most ancient procession: Jacob.

Remember the night Jacob spent using a stone for a pillow. God spoke to him, and in the morning Jacob erected the stone as a pillar and a memorial. He called the place Bethel, which means the "house of God" in Hebrew.

He declared that the stone would be (some translations say "become") the house of God (see Gen. 28:16-22).

Jacob called his entire extended family to "arise and go up [the typical word for religious procession] to Bethel" (Gen. 35:3). They go through an elaborate process of consecration which distinguishes this journey from ordinary nomadic wanderings (see Gen. 35:2-4). Another feature which marks this event as a grand procession under God's own leadership is the astounding wave of God's terror that fell on the cities surrounding their pathway to Bethel. It was a divine umbrella of protection from the potential enemies of Jacob's household (Gen. 35:5).

And they did meet with God as they established an altar for prolonged worship, experiencing His blessing, hearing His voice (see Gen. 35:6-15).

2. The great exodus: Moses and the tabernacle.

God's demand to Pharaoh to release His enslaved people is well known but frequently left incomplete. Never did God or Moses merely say, "Let my people go." Rather it was, "Let my people go, so that they may worship me" (Ex. 10:3, NIV). It was more than liberation. Their salvation was for the purpose of leading them to a place of worship. Though the physical procession led them out of Egypt toward the promised land, God was actually leading them to Himself, to a mountain where He dwelt and would meet with them. The song Moses sang in celebration of victory over Pharaoh's army is unmistakably clear in this matter:

> In your unfailing love you will lead the people
>   you have redeemed.
> In your strength you will guide them to your
>   holy dwelling....
> You will bring them in and plant them on the
>   mountain of your inheritance —

the place, O Lord, you made for your dwelling.
Exodus 15:13,17, NIV

Once again the surrounding nations are gripped by the trembling and dread, so the people of God "pass by" in safety to the place of worship which God has prepared for them (see Ex. 15:16, NIV).

As the Israelites camped in the wilderness, the focal point was always the tabernacle, a visual aid to teach and train God's people in the matter of approaching Him. It was described as a tent of meeting, once again displaying God's longing to be approached and served in the way which Moses exemplified — face-to-face.

3. David's tabernacle: unprecedented celebration.

After the years of apostasy and chaos in the time of the judges, King David resumes the interrupted procession. After a false start he successfully returns the ark of the covenant, the symbol of God's manifest presence, to Mount Zion, leading priests and people in a procession of unprecedented joy and celebration (see 2 Sam. 6:12-18). In a simplified tabernacle he inaugurates an era of prophetic praise, psalmody and thanksgiving twenty-four hours a day accompanied by singers, trumpeters and players of all kinds of stringed instruments. Yet David's heart reached prophetically for a greater fullness. He longed to build a greater and more permanent house in which to meet with God. God delayed David's plan and promised instead to use his son Solomon to build it. Though in time a physical temple is built, God made it clear that His full intention was to build an eternal house and an everlasting kingdom (see 2 Sam. 7:1-17, esp. v. 16).

4. The return of the exiles.

The people of God returned overtly to rebuild the temple of God. Prophets had sung generations earlier of their grand procession back to God's dwelling, bringing the nations with them. There was a rich expectation of return. Jonah said he looked again to the temple in his anguished prayer that was well remembered later during the exile (see Jon. 2:2-9). Isaiah and Micah had synchronized visions of the nations streaming to the mountain of God (see Is. 2 and Micah 4). Ezekiel was fixated on the building of a new temple of God. Isaiah is perhaps most rhapsodic about the joy of procession to God with the glory of nations (see Is. 60-66).

When the people of God arrived from captivity, they did more than build walls. They built the house of God. But it was frankly a disappointment to them. A prophetic faith would have to grip the people. God was urging them to look for the glory of a larger, greater, fuller house. This house lacked the baptism in glory and fire. It lacked the ark itself. But the spirit was abiding in their midst, just as at the exodus. The procession continues: Despise not days of small beginnings (see Zech. 4:10; for more about the Israelites' return from captivity, see Nehemiah, Ezra, Haggai and Zechariah).

Processions accompanied the building of the walls, notably when Nehemiah led the people in two processions, called thanksgivings. They marched in opposite directions on the top of the wall until they met, having encircled the city in a pincer movement. In contrast to Jericho, this was to establish walls of protection, not destroy walls of opposition.

God again provided defense as His people trekked together with the express purpose of building and beautifying God's house (Ezra 8:21-31). He moved the most powerful kings of the earth to offer an enduring protection from enemies who sought to frustrate the construction (Ezra 1 and 4-7). God even inspired the emperor Cyrus to call God's people to rise and rebuild the temple, using the explicit language of procession: "Whoever there is among you of all His people, may the Lord his God be with him, and let him go up!" (2 Chron. 36:23).

5. Jesus: the crescendo.

The climactic event of Jesus' life, intended as a crescendo, a grand public affair, was the triumphal march we have called Palm Sunday. It was a major affair, and we ought not to overlook it in the glory of His death and resurrection. What a mistake to focus on the crowds! What a mistake to make vapid points by saying the same people cheering Him would be jeering Him. Focus on Jesus. What did He do? Though He entered the city of Jerusalem, Jerusalem was not His destination. Where was He going? Where would He lead thousands? The house of God! Jesus was entering the temple, longing to be welcomed there.

The loud "hosannas" were but a refrain from the singing of Psalm 118, signalling the turning of the day of God, "the day the Lord has made," opening a new era in which the foundational cornerstone would be laid. This prophetic song speaks of the day in which the temple would be built on the stone of a Man, with all other stones being men and women alive with His life. He would come to this temple to the sound of praise as they cried out, "Blessed is He who comes in the name of the Lord!"

This grand procession was the fullest of all. All preceding processions were great and full, but this march was paramount, inaugurating the ultimate house of prayer for all peoples.

There is no mistaking that the worship of all nations was uppermost on Jesus' mind. As He entered and confronted what He found in the temple, He quoted and began extensive teaching from a key phrase of Isaiah 56:6-8. Surely He knew the rest of those verses: "Also the foreigners who joined themselves to the Lord...even those I will bring to My holy mountain, and make them joyful in My house of prayer. Their burnt offerings and their sacrifices will be acceptable on My altar; for My house will be called a house of prayer for all the peoples." Jesus was not thinking of encouraging better prayer meetings on behalf of the nations. He was recounting the ancient hope that every people would approach God in His house with an offering of worship.

As Jesus arrived in the temple, He surprised and amazed everyone. Was He building it or tearing it down? This question seemed to stand behind everything that happened during the final week of His life. He pronounced its certain destruction to His followers (Matt. 24:1-2) and more than hinted at its new founding on Himself to those that opposed Him (Matt. 21:42). He was finally brought to trial, under a garbled accusation of destroying and rebuilding the temple (see Matt. 27). Perhaps the question is still with us. Is Jesus rebuilding or tearing down? Let us behold our Lord carefully and hear what His prophetic actions say.

The Cleansing of the Temple

When Jesus entered the temple He branded it as a den of thieves and demonstrated in graphic prophetic acts God's displeasure at what was going on in His "house of prayer for all the nations." Jesus had quoted Jeremiah's call for repentance to the worshippers of His day, citing injustice; oppression of aliens, orphans and widows; the shedding of innocent blood; idolatry and an ugly catalogue of other sins (see Jer. 7). Worst of all, those who did these things were boasting in their religious heritage, arrogant and complacent. Let us be clear, however, that Jesus was not cleaning up the old physical temple in order to restore it to proper use. Rather He was exposing and judging its corruption and announcing its obsolescence.

It was a moment of judgment, and as such we can be very sure that such corruption has no place in the new temple of which He is the cornerstone.

Instead of making the temple a meeting place with God, calling the nations to come and be cleansed and bring their offerings, its custodians were intercepting the worshippers and extracting exorbitant percentages on their offerings. Instead of being a service to those who were seeking the face of God, their money exchange tables and stalls for selling sacrifices had become lucrative turnstiles obstructing the way. Significantly, this all took place in the courtyard of the Gentiles, ostensibly a place set aside for assisting seekers of God from the nations.

Jesus also refused to allow anyone to carry goods through the courtyard of the Gentiles. Apparently a short-cut existed through the temple courtyard and was used by people on their way to and from market (see Mark 11:16). There is an obvious lesson here. Many people will use the house of God as a convenience, not as a place of worship. They carry goods in their arms, but they are carrying them through. They are not presenting them at the altar as spiritual sacrifices for God's pleasure because they are trying to take a shortcut to somewhere else, seeking their own pleasure and profit. When Jesus comes to His temple, let us be sure that we are on the right side of the table. Let us be sure that He does not find us just passing through on our way to somewhere else.

A Taste of Fullness

Jesus immediately gave the entire city a taste of the dwelling of God with man. He taught them, and He touched them with healing (Luke 19:47).

> And the blind and the lame came to Him in the
> temple, and He healed them. But when the
> chief priests and the scribes saw the wonderful
> things that He had done, and the children who
> were crying out in the temple and saying,
> "Hosanna to the Son of David," they became
> indignant (Matt. 21:14-15).

The chief priests and their religious establishment had
marginalized the poor and the needy. In fact, Jesus' earlier
words seem to say the chief priests exploited the people.
Their rough interrogation of people whom Jesus had
healed illustrates their disdain for the commoners. Yet
when Jesus comes to the temple, common people flood
in after Him, and the blind and lame come to Him and
receive healing. The house of God is a place where Jesus
welcomes the outcasts and heals the sick.

Jesus not only received the outcast, He welcomed the
continued praise of the children who followed Him. The
children also were normally excluded but found a welcome with Jesus and exulted in it noisily. When complaints
were made He defended them, much I am sure to their
delight and further encouragement. " 'Yes,' replied Jesus,
'have you never read, "From the lips of children and
infants you have ordained praise"?' " (Matt. 21:16, NIV).

By receiving the children's praise, Jesus was judging
the worship of the temple. It had become legalistic, formal and oppressive. The ministers had become censorious. There was no room for childlike joy and exuberance.
But, according to Jesus, the praise the children brought
was prepared or ordained by God for Himself — simple,
noisy, joyful, spontaneous, unsophisticated as it was.

The context of the psalm which Jesus quoted here
brings us back as well to the previous pattern of God
establishing a defense for those approaching Him in

procession. In Psalm 8 the children's praise makes "the enemy and the revengeful cease" (Ps. 8:2). As it is rendered elsewhere, children's worship silences the foe and the avenger. This is remarkably consistent with all previous processions toward God's house of worship, when the dread of God falls upon aggressors and results in a safe passage through for the worshippers. In the innocent festivity of praising children God is dealing with powerful enemies. And the beauty of it is that all this is going on unseen while Jesus remains the focus of attention.

I have seen many children participate in praise marches. They love the excitement, the movement, the color, the music and the fact they can participate. They can understand the simple motive of loving Jesus and making Him known. Plus they can make as much noise as they want to! But much more than this, I have observed how children instinctively catch in their spirits the significance of public praise, especially marches. While on one level it is a lot of fun, on another level many seem to take it very seriously.

Jesus recognized the praise from the children on Palm Sunday as ordained by God, and He endorsed its prophetic content. Today children are also gathering to Jesus, where in His spiritual house of worship He delights to receive their praises. Let us not hinder them but rather equip, encourage and release them into the fullness of being a generation that earnestly seeks the glory of God in the face of Jesus.

The Temple Built From All Nations

Now there were certain Greeks among those who were going up to worship at the feast; these therefore came to Philip, who was from Bethsaida of Galilee, and began to ask him, saying, "Sir, we wish to see Jesus" (John 12:20-21).

The answer Jesus gave when His disciples reported this seems at first obtuse: "The hour has come for the Son of Man to be glorified" (John 12:23). He was speaking of His death, but it seems that this report in some way signalled its rapid approach. The clue is in the words that followed shortly afterward: "And I, if I be lifted up from the earth, will draw all men to Myself" (John 12:32). That Gentiles were seeking Jesus was a signal that the inauguration of the house of prayer for all nations was truly underway. It was time for this new building to be filled with glory, the glory of the Son of Man, which burned most brightly in His suffering.

My point is this: At this time we are nearing the completion of the greatest temple, the temple made without hands. God will flood that dwelling with great glory. Through Christ, believers are being fitted together, growing into a holy temple unto the Lord (see Eph. 2:20-22). We are being built as living stones. But one condition is clear: We must come to Him. As Peter writes, "Coming to Him...you...are being built up as a spiritual house" (1 Pet. 2:4-5). Peter's choice of the word *come* indicates a sense of procession. God builds as we come.

This house stands incomplete without the nations. The request of the foreigners at Jesus' praise march is so very telling: "We want to see Jesus." The nations want so very much to see Jesus.

Let us march for Jesus in such a way that we march *with* Jesus, making Him the point of it all. How can we doubt that the nations will come to Him and fill His house with glory?

TWELVE

SPIRITUAL SACRIFICES

And coming to Him as to a living stone, rejected by men, but choice and precious in the sight of God, you also, as living stones, are being built up as a spiritual house for a holy priesthood, to offer up spiritual sacrifices acceptable to God through Jesus Christ (1 Pet. 2:4-5).

We have begun to establish an understanding of the purpose and meaning of actual marches and public praise events. Alongside their growth we have observed what seems to be the unfolding of a wider vision that includes them but at the same time transcends them. The phenomenon of marches on an international scale, synchronized more by relationship around a shared vision than by complex coordination, lends it more of an atmosphere of a movement than merely the popularization of a method. Truths are being modeled; spiritual realities are taking on physical manifestations.

We have noted the powerful symbolism and prophetic significance of the destination of Jesus' march, the temple. At the temple, Jesus reaffirmed that God's purpose has always been to build a house of prayer for all nations. We have recognized that this house of prayer, this temple, is not made of physical stones. This is a spiritual house made of living stones built around Jesus, the choice and precious cornerstone. We have established that Jesus who shows us the Father is the main attraction. All the various components, benefits and spin-offs of marching for Jesus can be summed up in three words from Peter's epistle: We are "coming to Him."

But when we come to Him, how do we do it? How do we express our devotion? What happens in this spiritual house? First, we are not talking about a conceptual house, an abstract idea, rich in imagery but unsubstantial. The imagery is to help us to understand a spiritual reality even more solid than bricks and beams. The symbol is there to bring the substance to light.

God is building a house on the earth because He desires to dwell among His people. When He chose a nation through which to make Himself known, He required that they build a tabernacle, a tent, as a meeting place with them. It was only because of their sinfulness that God in His mercy required the tabernacle to be situated outside the camp, lest His holy presence destroy them. Though the people only entered the outer courts, Moses and Aaron stepped into the holy of holies and enjoyed a more personal encounter.

Now our feet step in holy fear over the threshold of a spiritual house that God is building on the earth out of living stones hewn from the quarry of every tribe, nation and tongue. As we come we must approach in the splendor of holiness because only a holy priesthood can survive such purity. The job of the old Mosaic priesthood was to offer sacrifices acceptable to God. As priests of the new covenant we do not come empty-handed but bring spiritual sacrifices acceptable to God through Jesus Christ. Now that the blood of Jesus Himself has been offered once and for all as a sacrifice to atone for our sins, there is no need for any more blood to be shed. The day of animal sacrifice is long past. Besides, animal sacrifices could never wipe out the record of our guilt and wrong-doing. The greatest sacrifice of all has been made, and it is a total gift to us, who deserve only judgment but have received mercy.

In celebration of the Lamb who was slain and of His stupendous love, we are invited to stream into His holy presence, our arms laden with spiritual sacrifices, lavishing gifts upon Him with unbounded affection. So what are the spiritual sacrifices that we are privileged to bring? In the Scriptures, eight are listed. Though they are termed "spiritual," they illustrate the utterly practical nature of the spirituality we are called to practice in the presence of the Lord.

Presenting Our Bodies

Paul urges the Roman church of his day to respond to God's mercies by presenting "your bodies [as] a living and holy sacrifice, acceptable to God, which is your spiritual service of worship" (Rom. 12:1). Spirituality, as I have said, is utterly practical. So, of course, Paul explains what behavior is or is not consistent with the acceptability of that living and holy sacrifice. We are to be transformed by the renewing of our minds rather than conformed by the standards of this world. Within a few sentences he is exhorting all to exercise their different gifts within the body of Christ for the common good and with the purest motivation.

We can go nowhere until we have knelt here, at the place where we lay down our own lives, our own interests, in grateful response to God for His great mercies. Worship is indeed our new way of life as we bring all we are, all we have and all we do, and live it all and do it all for Him. Worship as a new way of life is validated in the context of our relationships within the church, the body of Christ. In the spiritual house we are building, the bricks that are beside, above and below us are our Christian brothers and sisters.

The Fruit of Our Lips

The writer to the Hebrews described Christ through the types and shadows of old covenant temple worship. Having established Jesus as the great high priest who has opened the way for us into the holy of holies, he writes, "Through Him then, let us continually offer up a sacrifice of praise to God, that is, the fruit of lips that give thanks to His name" (Heb. 13:15). So the holy priesthood comes in ceaseless procession, in perpetual praise, in continual thanksgiving. The praise is felt internally, but it is also vocalized, the fruit of our lips noising abroad His greatness.

We have reminded ourselves that the temple is not the church building, that "the Most High does not dwell in houses made by human hands" (Acts 7:48). But we also know that He says, "Heaven is My throne, and earth is the footstool of My feet" (Acts 7:49). Is it not obvious that, as a holy priesthood worshipping such a God, our procession of worship is truly in a cosmic dimension? This continual praise which rises to fill all heaven and earth cannot be contained by man-made walls or borders.

At the peak of his reign, King David, the man after God's own heart, instituted a system of around-the-clock praise on a grand scale. Today, in every time zone, twenty-four hours a day, the sound of praise is continually ascending before God, a growing crescendo out of many tribes and nations.

John's vision in the book of Revelation illustrates the third spiritual sacrifice, once again in the typology of temple worship. "And another angel came and stood at the altar, holding a golden censer; and much incense was given to him, that he might add it to the prayers of all the saints upon the golden altar which was before the throne. And the smoke of the incense, with the prayers of the saints, went up before God out of the angel's hand" (Rev. 8:3-4). Similarly the twenty-four elders in worship before the Lamb have "golden bowls full of incense, which are the prayers of the saints" (Rev. 5:8).

Prayer

Our prayers are spiritual sacrifices, offered in the spiritual house of God, and they have an awesome effect upon the world. "And the angel took the censer; and he filled it with the fire of the altar and threw it to the earth; and there followed peals of thunder and sounds and flashes of lightning and an earthquake" (Rev. 8:5). The prayers precipitated the coming of the judgments of God upon the earth.

A Broken and Contrite Heart

The next spiritual sacrifice is a reminder of the tenderness and gentleness of the God to whom we are bringing our offering. It is described in David's psalm of penitence as he repented from committing adultery with Bathsheba and having her husband killed on the battlefield. "The sacrifices of God are a broken spirit; a broken and contrite heart, O God, you will not despise" (Ps. 51:17, NIV).

In the midst of repentance and sorrow we can confidently offer before Him our brokenness, humbled and overawed by His amazing grace. Even though there is much joy to bring (in the same psalm David prays for the joy of his salvation to be restored), we do not have to wait for joy before we can worship. We can bring our tears, our contriteness, our sorrow knowing that God will never despise such offerings. A sinful woman, probably a prostitute, washed Jesus' feet with her tears. He accepted her worship, rebuking her critics by illustrating with a parable that those who have been forgiven much, love much. Paul speaks of serving the Lord with tears (Acts 20:19). The Lord saw Hezekiah's tears and heard his prayers and gave him fifteen more years to live (Is. 38:5).

Jesus, our great high priest, wept as He stood looking out over Jerusalem. Describing this aspect of His priesthood, the writer to the Hebrews reports, "In the days of His flesh, He offered up both prayers and supplications with loud crying and tears" (Heb. 5:7). All that Jesus said and did was said and done as a priest in the presence of His Father before His altar. In Gethsemane, though physically He was in a garden just outside Jerusalem, as high priest He was before the throne of the Most High God. There He brought His broken heart and agonized spirit and offered them with tears. As we come to Him in His temple, tears are gifts He will not despise.

Our Lives Poured Out

The apostle Paul tells the Philippians, "But even if I am being poured out as a drink offering upon the sacrifice and service of your faith, I rejoice and share my joy with you all" (Phil. 2:17). Here we find two further spiritual sacrifices. First, Paul is likening his own ministry to the Philippians to the drink offerings, sometimes called libations, of oil and wine which were to accompany the daily offering of lambs to God in the tabernacle (see Ex. 29:40-41). These daily offerings were designed to be of fundamental pleasure to God. They were not considered to be sacrifices atoning for sins because other specific sacrifices provided for that. The daily offerings and the drink offerings which accompanied them were directly associated with God's desire to meet and speak with His people (see Ex. 29:41).

We can see then how Paul must have valued the daily service that the Philippians gave God. He considered himself to be an accompaniment. They were the main event. Paul had every reason to suppose that he would soon die. But the Philippian service would go on, established, thriving, in full flame of faith for God's pleasure. He thought it a deep joy of eternal significance to serve as an igniting catalyst for their fruitful labor to stand complete on the day of Christ.

This spiritual offering is difficult but delightful. It is the sacrifice of enhancing and strengthening the others' service to God without concern for notoriety or prominence. All such gifts come into glorious light on the day of Christ's coming (see Phil. 2:16).

Dedicated servants of God today can take deep joy in their labor to strengthen the service others give to God, whether their efforts are duly recognized or not. Who hasn't felt their work at some time to be "poured out" and wasted? Labor for others is not at all squandered if it is personally offered to God. Who is willing, like Paul, to serve alongside others who may be positioned in a more prominent light? How is it possible to build up the ministry of others without regard for immediate reward and honor? Paul found deep joy in pouring himself out for others' work because they produced enduring fruit for God.

In 2 Timothy 4:5-6 we see the same, wonderful self-emptying. The drink offering refers to martyrdom in a most intimate way. Paul urged young coworker Timothy to fulfill his ministry, which was being accomplished by joining forces with Paul. Why did Paul encourage Timothy to complete his work? Paul points to his own eminent death as a drink offering for the fulfillment of Timothy's work yet to come. Nothing more intimate and tender could be imagined. "For I am already being poured out as a drink offering, and the time of my departure has come."

Acts of Faith

Paul goes on to describe the Philippians' faith as generating a "sacrifice and service" (Phil. 2:17). He is gladly pouring out his own life on top of their own sacrifices. If we do not normally think of faith as bringing forth a worship offering, then perhaps we should begin by reading Hebrews 11 where the heroes of faith are celebrated. The chapter begins with Abel who "by faith...offered to God a better sacrifice than Cain, through which he obtained the testimony that he was righteous, God testifying about his gifts, and through faith, though he is dead, he still speaks" (Heb. 11:4). The list continues with men and women who were worshippers and whose faith manifested itself in outstanding sacrifice and service.

We are to be worshippers not only by means of words, but by virtue of acts of faith. Many of them will be costly to us, but they are received as precious by the Lord. Indeed, it is impossible to worship at all unless we have faith, for it is by faith we believe God exists and can be approached through Christ.

Doing Good and Sharing

Following immediately after the exhortation to bring the "fruit of our lips" as a continual sacrifice of praise to God is another pleasing sacrifice: "Do not neglect doing good and sharing; for with such sacrifices God is pleased"

(Heb. 13:16). The imagery is still that of temple worship, bringing to the altar acceptable sacrifices. Yet these are not predominantly church service activities. Doing good and sharing are best worked out in day-to-day living, often in terms of material needs or practical care. Nevertheless, they are being received as part of the worship in God's spiritual house of worship, if indeed we do not neglect to do such things. Why do we persist in trying to separate the practical and the spiritual or to elevate one above the other? The fruit of our lips, good deeds and sharing what we have — all these are pleasing acts of worship before the throne of God. After all, if we are clear about practical expressions of love, we should know that whatever we do for the least of Jesus' loved ones, we do for Him.

Financial Giving

Paul accepted a substantial financial gift from the Philippians. "I have received...from Epaphroditus what you have sent, a fragrant aroma, an acceptable sacrifice, well-pleasing to God" (Phil. 4:18). Paul almost overdoes the language of the temple sacrifices in describing their gift. Though he had no immediate need for money, Paul knew the gift was of vast value before God. This was not a flowery word of gratitude. Paul was trying to encourage the Philippians to lavish themselves upon God in every way and not merely to measure their financial lives by the perceived urgency of needs they might encounter.

He had described elsewhere the Philippian church as those who "gave themselves first to the Lord and then to us" (2 Cor. 8:5, NIV). This makes a wonderful point about our financial lives before God. In giving to others, we also offer gifts to God. In this way, financial stewardship takes on a lovely, heavenly dimension.

The Offering of the Nations

Not surprisingly, the eighth spiritual sacrifice is also brought to us by courtesy of Paul. As a Pharisee of Pharisees, he was steeped in the knowledge of temple worship. He describes the grace given him from God "to be a minister of Christ Jesus to the Gentiles, ministering as a priest the gospel of God, that my offering of the Gentiles might become acceptable, sanctified by the Holy Spirit" (Rom. 15:16).

Though his church planting had taken him zigzagging around the Roman empire, in marketplaces, auditoriums and homes, in the spirit his ministry was taking place in the spiritual temple. He knew that his preaching of the gospel was a priestly duty. Though he stood before people, he knew that invisibly he was "priesting the gospel" before the mercy seat, the throne of God where the sprinkled blood speaks of Jesus' atoning sacrifice.* But look at the offering this priest is bringing. This time the offering is not praise or prayers or faith or good deeds. It is people and the nations.** His job is to prepare them, like a priest prepares an offering, to be acceptable to God and sanctified by the Holy Spirit. Let me shout it loud and clear: Evangelism is worship. Church planting is worship. It is all a priestly duty and privilege. And it is all happening in the temple being built with living stones, of which Jesus Christ is the chief cornerstone.

Paul had one supreme motive for his extraordinary labors of love as he planted churches and carried the burden of them through his difficult life. He was bringing

---

* The phrase "priesting the gospel" reflects a literal translation of the original Greek.
** The Greek word in Romans 15:16 is *ethnos*, commonly translated as Gentiles or nations.

love-gifts to God. His life-style could have been motivated by lesser things — by personal ambition, by needs, by obligation, by pressure, by habit, by rivalry, by greed, by good intentions or by sympathy for the lost. But Paul dignified, purified and elevated it into a priestly ministry by his desire to bring to God what pleases Him. There are two things that God is described as seeking. One is the lost. The other is true worshippers. Let's bring them both together in one package!

The Moravians

The supreme motive of bringing the glory of the people to God gave Paul a practical focus for his mission efforts as well. He aspired to labor where Christ was not yet named — where Christ was not worshipped, obeyed and exalted. Paul's empowering vision was to see representatives from all the peoples worshipping God in Christ's name. Taking that as our mission, will we long delay from the difficult labor to be done among the peoples yet to see or hear the gospel? (See Rom. 15:18-21.) Such pure passion has fueled and focused mission efforts before.

A good example is a small evangelistic movement that emerged during the eighteenth century from a small refugee community in Herrnhut, a town in Saxony, Germany. Within a single decade it had become a center of missionary and evangelistic endeavor operating on a worldwide scale. Led by Count Nikolaus Ludwig von Zinzendorf, the community founded what became known as the Moravian church. The movement was characterized by sacrificial love and service to Christ, prayer and mission. In Herrnhut, twenty-four-hour prayer meetings were begun, which continued without interruption for more than one hundred years. Many regard this movement as the birthplace of modern-day missions, and many of their exploits have a legendary quality about them.

In 1731, Count Zinzendorf met a Negro slave called Anthony who came from St. Thomas in the Danish West Indies. The man was working in the Royal Court and had been converted. He told Zinzendorf how the slaves lived in appalling conditions of poverty and disease, and they desperately needed to hear the gospel. Zinzendorf brought the report back to Herrnhut and arranged for Anthony to come to the Moravian community a few weeks later. The report had such an effect on a young man called Leonhard Dober that he immediately determined to offer himself to serve those oppressed and enslaved people.

When Anthony arrived and spoke to the community, he said that it was his belief that the only way possible for a missionary to reach the slaves in St. Thomas was to become a slave himself. That was because the slaves worked all day on the plantations and were kept by a strict curfew in their huts at night. Only by working alongside them in the sugarcane fields could anyone hope to have a chance of sharing the gospel. This daunting prospect did not discourage Dober. Sometime later, he and David Nitschmann, who had similarly offered himself, set off for St. Thomas. With virtually no money in their purses they headed to Copenhagen to get a ship to the West Indies. When they shared their plans with other people, they were laughed at. When they said they were *prepared to work as slaves* if necessary, everyone thought they were mad!

In December 1732 they sighted St. Thomas from the ship on which they had worked their passage. It was at this moment that Dober is believed to have turned to Nitschmann and said, "Let us give to the Lamb the reward for His sufferings." When I first heard this story and these words, my spirit was profoundly stirred. It was not just their selflessness and courage, not even their willingness to become slaves if necessary, that moved me, though that was awe-inspiring. It was the motive expressed in those few words.

For me it was a moment of truth, as I saw more clearly than ever before that worship and mission are essentially the same thing. There are endless good and noble reasons for taking the good news to the ends of the earth, but the best is this: to give to Christ, the Lamb of God, the reward for His sufferings.

Though as events unfolded they were not called upon to become slaves, their sufferings were severe. Out of the group of eighteen more Moravians who joined them on the island, eight had died from disease within a year. Yet they labored sacrificially through violent and sometimes murderous opposition from vested interests among the colonial authorities. As a result, thirteen thousand slaves were converted and baptized in the West Indies before any other missions began there.

An early Moravian hymn has this line which is typical of their mission motive:

> Glad, we bear want and distress
> to set forth the Lamb once slain.

This is reminiscent of the new song which the four living creatures and the twenty-four elders sing before the Lamb in the book of Revelation. They proclaim His worthiness because He gave up His life and with His blood purchased for God people from every tribe and tongue and nation. Should we deny Him what He has already purchased at such a price? He endured the cross and despised the shame for the joy set before Him, the joy of bringing people like us to the Father. Will we then rob Him of some of that joy? What better act of worship could we possibly bring Him than people, redeemed out of every tribe and tongue and nation, as a crown for the end of the ages'?

Righteousness and Praise

> For as the earth brings forth its sprouts, and as a garden causes the things sown in it to spring up, so the Lord God will cause righteousness and praise to spring up before all the nations. For Zion's sake I will not keep silent, and for Jerusalem's sake I will not keep quiet, until her righteousness goes forth like brightness, and her salvation like a torch that is burning. And the nations will see your righteousness, and all kings your glory (Is. 61:11-62:2).

It is clear from our brief study of these eight spiritual sacrifices that as a holy priesthood we are to bring the whole of our lives to God as an act of worship. When praise springs up before neighborhoods, cities or nations, it must not spring up alone. True praise is never just songs. It is the overflow of a new society in Christ, and that society is characterized by righteousness. Praise and righteousness go together.

In the course of my earlier attempts to write music specifically for the streets, I studied the early history of the Salvation Army as an historical model out of which I might gain some ideas, some inspiration, some principles. One of the things that struck me most forcibly was the way in which they combined their public exhibition of praise, prayer and proclamation with social action. William Booth's vision was for the rescue of the whole society not just for the salvation of souls. They combined their street work with their praise processions. Even before handing over a loaf of bread to an impoverished household, they would sing a hymn and perhaps give a short gospel address. Their social action, their preaching, their prayer and their public praise all flowed together as one.

That was about the same time I was struck by the verse from Isaiah: "For as the earth brings forth its sprouts, and as a garden causes the things sown in it to spring up, so the Lord God will cause righteousness and praise to spring up before all the nations" (Is. 61:11). What struck me was this combination of righteousness and praise. When I looked at the history of the Salvation Army, I saw these two things standing side by side. I began to wonder how much the movement might have been inhibited if one or the other of those factors had not been present. Would praise and preaching on the streets without the righteous acts of mercy and kindness have become hollow, empty and irrelevant to the slum dwellers among whom they were working? Would social action without praise, prayer and proclamation have robbed them of the spiritual power which transformed lives and turned drunkards into caring parents?

The necessary blend of social action with spiritual power was one of the challenges levelled at March for Jesus in the early days. When we made a great demonstration on the streets through praise, people wondered whether we were actually avoiding issues within our society that needed action on a social and political level. Some had judged that we were over-spiritualizing the problems of our cities and neighborhoods and were unwilling to get our hands dirty in practical expressions of Christian love, choosing a soft option. What they seemed to forget was that the three groups which had initiated the march had been deeply involved in areas of social action for many years and continued to pour themselves into such.

Our view was that the integrity of the marches lay in the love and sacrifice which were being poured out through the regular ministry of the rank and file of our people all year. The special "festival" days on which we invade the streets have to be seen against the background of the 365 days during which the spiritual battle is being fought upon many different fronts.

In the eighteenth century an extraordinary period of spiritual revival took place under the ministry of John and Charles Wesley. Wesley is known well for his journal and his outdoor preaching. Charles is famous for his hymns. However, few people know the way in which the Methodist movement attacked evil within society on an intensely practical level. They founded schools and hospitals and were active in places of employment. They even campaigned for the abolition of slavery. At that time, ordinary people suffered poor health because they did not have money to pay for doctors. Out of concern for this, John wrote a medical handbook with the intention of putting it into the hands of ordinary people and easing their suffering. One of the quainter cures within this journal was apparently a remedy for baldness which involved rubbing garlic into the affected areas. It didn't appear to work, but it certainly gave the sufferer a lot of time on his own!

In his book *God's Strategy in Human History*, Roger Forster quotes the secular historian Howes, who said evangelical Christians brought about the majority of the social reform in the period. Righteousness and praise must always stand together. Righteousness without praise can tend toward activism without the benefit of the Holy Spirit's power. Praise without righteousness can tend toward triumphalism, an empty noise without power.

Both virtues in isolation are in danger of becoming actions without love — no better than clanging gongs and tinkling cymbals (see 1 Cor. 13).

A friend who recently visited San Francisco told me about taking part in an innovative street event. A group of Christians from a predominantly black church had organized what they termed a block party. Choosing a depressed and deprived housing area, they obtained permission from the authorities to shut off several streets. This freed an intersection from traffic and created a large, open space. Along one side of the intersection they set up a stage for a praise band. Along another side of the square they set up a food line and prepared to distribute clothes and groceries to meet the practical needs of the people who lived there. As the music began, creating a joyful party atmosphere, people were drawn from their houses where many felt trapped by the violence prevalent in the area. Then the group invited them to feast on the good things of the kingdom of God both material and spiritual. My friend reported that a number of people were converted, and many more received prayer and various kinds of ministry.

This passage in Isaiah reminds us that righteousness springs up because the Sovereign Lord causes it to happen. As the rain irrigates the soil, so righteousness from heaven refreshes the earth. Like a garden in spring time, the seeds long hidden underground sprout and become gloriously visible.

The same theme runs elsewhere in Isaiah. For example: "Drip down, O heavens, from above, and let the clouds pour down righteousness; let the earth open up and salvation bear fruit, and righteousness spring up with it. I, the Lord, have created it" (Is. 45:8). We can conclude that there is no true righteousness except that which comes from heaven. The Lord Himself is our righteousness. The apostle Paul takes up this theme in Romans: "For in the gospel a righteousness from God is revealed, a righteousness that is by faith from first to last" (Rom. 1:17, NIV).

In the imagery of Isaiah 61:11 God's righteousness raining down upon the earth causes righteousness to spring up from the earth. This important truth shows we cannot generate true righteousness on a purely horizontal level by human effort. True righteousness comes from heaven out of our relationship with the God who Himself is our righteousness. Righteousness overflows out of our daily relationship with Him.

I have seen tremendous results in movements that have combined righteousness and praise. This could explain why our arch enemy, Satan, seems to work very hard to separate the two. My own personal observation is that movements tend to swing one way or the other. Groups polarize between an emphasis on righteousness and an emphasis on praise. Those who gravitate toward Christian activism in the pursuit of political and social change sometimes neglect worship and prayer. At the other extreme there are many who prefer to pursue purely spiritual activities. They consume all their time and energy in hymn singing and prayer meetings and don't seem to notice the suffering around them.

Spiritual activities can become an escape from the costly demands of the real world of need around us. The story is told of some parishioners that arrived at their local church for worship one morning to discover the doors locked and bolted. The vicar had posted a notice at the entrance: "You have been coming here long enough. Now go and do it!"

In Western culture I believe that we suffer from the idea religion can be a private activity set apart in a compartment of its own and having little or nothing to do with the way in which we live our daily lives. Even though the great apostle Peter experienced the Holy Spirit at Pentecost, he needed to be reminded to incorporate his faith into all areas of his life. Paul had to rebuke him for racism, as he and other leaders from Jerusalem refused to eat with Gentile converts. Peter went through many struggles with the challenge of accepting Gentiles into the church (see Gal. 2:11-21).

We must not imagine we can dwell in God's presence without a practical outworking of righteousness. David writes, "O Lord, who may abide in Thy tent? Who may dwell on Thy holy hill? He who walks with integrity, and works righteousness" (Ps. 15:1-2). We may be very familiar with Hebrews 13:15, which says, "Through Him then, let us continually offer up a sacrifice of praise to God, that is, the fruit of lips that give thanks to His name." We may not be quite so familiar with the subsequent verse: "And do not neglect doing good and sharing; for with such sacrifices God is pleased" (Heb. 13:16). The fruit of our lips is not the whole story of the kind of worship which is acceptable to God.

As well as issues of personal righteousness, we need to recognize that we cannot isolate our Christian expression of praise from what could be called corporate righteousness. In other words, we should confront such corporate issues of unrighteousness in societies as materialism, racism, sexism and nationalism. For example, the Corinthian church was very charismatic but managed to neglect the poor and tolerate inequalities even in the celebration of the Lord's supper (1 Cor. 11:18-34). John Stott, a well-known British Bible teacher, says, "Christians cannot regard with equanimity the injustices which spoil God's world and demean his creatures. Injustice must bring pain to the God whose justice flared brightly at the cross. It should bring pain to God's people too."

There is danger in giving every question a spiritual answer rather than attacking it at its point of manifestation in society. Sometimes the spiritual and the social seem to converge in a dramatic way, for example, when the Salvation Army took up the issue of child prostitution in 1885.

A new convert, Rebecca Jarrett, a thirty-six-year-old ex-drunkard and brothel-keeper for twenty years, was grieved by the trafficking in children. She, along with William T. Stead, who was a famous London editor, and the Salvation Army, launched a fantastic plot to confirm, expose and end children's slave traffic. The campaign eventually embroiled the army in bitter controversy. It resulted not in the arrest and conviction of the child traders, but of the two leaders of the opposition!

Rebecca Jarrett had posed as a procurer and William Stead as "one of the wealthy debauchers to whom so many hundreds of the children of the poor were annually sacrificed." Obtaining a pretty child called Eliza Armstrong for two pounds from her mother, they documented the entire process in the July 6, 1885, issue of the *Pall Mall Gazette*. It "took the British public by storm, in a way that can hardly be paralleled in newspaper history." Where it was opposed, young Bernard Shaw himself offered to go out and sell the paper. Where it was in demand, enterprising newsboys sold the last copies at exorbitant prices.

The "dead" Criminal Law Amendment Bill was suddenly resurrected before a packed and excited house of Parliament. Within seventeen days, more than 343,000 signatures filled the Salvation Army's monster petition to the House of Commons. Two miles in length, the petition was carried by eight Salvationists onto the floor of the house. In a month, the bill was law, and the age of consent was raised to sixteen. But the underworld, outraged at their exposure, counterattacked. They took William Stead and Rebecca Jarrett to court indicting them under an 1861 abduction act! This "most sensational trial of the nineteenth century" ended with Stead and Ms. Jarrett respectively receiving three- and six-month sentences. They had succeeded. It cost them all dearly, but they broke the back of one of the most vile and vicious practices in England's history.[1]

In joyful procession, an army of worshippers had brought the Savior they loved a most precious offering — a purer and more just society and a legacy of protection for the weak which has benefitted several generations since. He is worthy of countless more such offerings and will receive them as righteousness and praise spring up before all nations.

THIRTEEN

No Quick Fix

The Earth Is the Lord's

As a young teenager brought up in the evangelical tradition I had unconsciously adopted a peculiar view of events outside the Christian scene — the scene that was in many ways my little world. I can remember articulating this in a discussion about some matter of national significance. The essence of my view was, You can't change anything. It's all too big for us, and we have no significance as Christians. It's not even worth trying.

Perhaps to some degree this was the emotion of a young person facing a world which was not only perplexing but was evidently run by adults. Yet my words also reflected the mood of much of the evangelical church at that time. Churchgoing was declining drastically. Christian morality was definitely going out of fashion. Sex, drugs and rock 'n' roll were in fashion, against which background the churches seemed to have lost their relevance, their confidence and their spiritual power. Any idea of a kind of Christianity that could change the course of a nation's history was confined to memories of a glorious past.

Yet the reality is that by His incarnation, death, resurrection and ascension, Jesus has already changed everything. While we are waiting for Him to act, He is waiting for us. His intervention into our world is a completed work. In His dying agonies He cried out, "It is finished," and afterward ascended to heaven. We are told that He sat down at the right hand of the Father, indicating that as both sacrificial Lamb and great high priest, the once-and-for-all sacrifice for sins had been made, and heaven's door was thrown open.

Praise marching emboldens saints to believe that both they and their world not only can change but must indeed be transformed. And it could be that if believers sag back from this simple, resilient hope, public praise becomes a hollow affair. For some the praise march may turn sour into a nasty triumphalism. For others it may become thin and evaporate like any other fad. But for those who urgently lay hold of a glad certainty that God even now is making all things new, joy increases with a beautiful sobriety.

A psalm which has had great relevance to this and has helped in my pursuit of understanding praise marches is Psalm 24. It is thought to have been written by King David when the ark of the covenant was returned to Mount Zion in Jerusalem. An extraordinarily joyful procession marked the establishment of David's tabernacle followed by an unprecedented era of extravagant praise, coinciding with the greatest period of David's reign. As they approached the city gates, ascending the incline, the singers in the procession would cry out, "Lift up your heads, O gates...that the King of glory may come in!" (Ps. 24:7). Those on the city walls would reply, "Who is this King of glory?" (v. 10). And so the responsive shouts would begin.

This psalm has long been accepted as a prophetic foreshadowing of the ascension of the risen Christ. It portrays a scene of tumultuous welcome as He arrives at the gates of the heavenly Jerusalem, fresh from His victory on the cross, welcomed by the sound of proclamation and praise bouncing antiphonally between heaven and earth. Despite its relative briefness, this psalm is rich and deep in meaning, and every layer peeled off reveals another and yet another.

> The earth is the Lord's, and all it contains,
> The world, and those who dwell in it.
> For He has founded it upon the seas,
> And established it upon the rivers.
> Who may ascend into the hill of the Lord?
> And who may stand in His holy place?
> He who has clean hands and a pure heart,
> Who has not lifted up his soul to falsehood,
> And has not sworn deceitfully.
> He shall receive a blessing from the Lord
> And righteousness from the God of his salva-
>   tion.
> This is the generation of those who seek Him,
> Who seek Thy face — even Jacob.
> > Selah.
>
> Lift up your heads, O gates,
> And be lifted up, O ancient doors,
> That the King of glory may come in!
> Who is the King of glory?
> The Lord strong and mighty,

> The Lord mighty in battle.
> Lift up your heads, O gates,
> And lift them up, O ancient doors,
> That the King of glory may come in!
> Who is this King of glory?
> The Lord of hosts,
> He is the King of glory.
>
> Psalm 24

First, He has ascended to the highest throne of the universe, where He has sat down to reign. There is no higher position, no place of greater power authority or dominion. Second, He has gone ahead of us in order to lead us there as a holy priesthood to worship Him and reign with Him forever.

All Doors Are Open

If the gates of heaven itself are flung wide to receive the victorious risen Christ, then it means that every other gate or door first had to make way for Him. His victory procession began when at His death, He descended into the place of the dead, stormed its gates, took the keys of death and hell from the devil and announced His victory there (see Rev. 1:18). Then having plundered hell He marched back to life by the power of the Holy Spirit, leading His victory procession.

After spending time strengthening His disciples He kept on going, ascending to the Father's side:

> When He ascended on high, He led captive a host of captives, and He gave gifts to men. (Now this expression, "He ascended," what does it mean except that He also had descended into the lower parts of the earth? He who de-

scended is Himself also He who ascended far
above all the heavens, that He might fill all
things) (Eph. 4:8-10).

The procession of Jesus has marched from death to
life, from deepest darkness to pure unbearable light, from
hell to heaven. Along the way astounded archangels and
terrified demon-rulers have fallen in submission as His
wounded feet have passed by. Beginning with the keys of
death and hell, He has collected every other key and
opened every other door along the way. Beginning with
Satan himself, He has disarmed every evil power and
taken them captive, displaying them as trophies of His
cosmic battle.

But those who follow Christ faithfully are also in this
procession. As Paul struggles with leading the church at
Corinth, he takes up the imagery of procession and says,
"But thanks be to God, who always leads us in His
triumph in Christ, and manifests through us the sweet
aroma of the knowledge of Him in every place" (2 Cor.
2:14).

Christ's ascension means that if heaven and hell have
been traversed, all doors have been flung open, all veils
torn, all keys handed over, all dividing walls broken
down. There is no place on His earth He cannot and will
not go and fill with His glorious presence. Truly, all the
earth shall be filled with the knowledge of the glory of
the Lord as the waters cover the sea. Truly the earth is the
Lord's and everything that is in it.

What a contrast this is to the mood of fatalistic accep-
tance which seeped into my soul at so young an age! God
had to revive my spirit, re-educate my mind and reorient
my worldview. I can remember the period of my life when
He began to deal with my passivity. As was normal, it
eventually came out in songs, notably one titled "God Put

a Fighter in Me." It contained the stanza:

> Where have all the Christian soldiers gone?
> Where is the resistance — will no one be
> strong?
> When will we stand up tall and straight —
> Rise up and storm the gates?

Not only do we have abundant confidence that our world will change, but we can be sure that we are the very kind of people that God desires to come near Him in priestly purity. God is not teasing or taunting us. Christ's triumph means He will win us over to Himself as well, bringing about a substantial change of character. The purity He desires He is well able to work within us.

Holiness Required

As Psalm 24 says, those who intend to ascend the hill of the Lord and "stand in His holy place" (v. 3) must come in the splendor of holiness required of the priests of old: clean hands, a pure heart, truth in the secret inner life of the soul, blameless in speech. This characterizes the generations of "those who seek Him...even Jacob" (v. 6). The mention of Jacob seems at first curious. What should this generation have in common with Jacob? The quality in Jacob which won his favor with God, despite the deviousness of his earlier life, was his tenacity in seeking the face of God. Remember his wrestling match with the angel?

> Then he [the angel] said, "Let me go, for the dawn is breaking." But he [Jacob] said, "I will not let you go unless you bless me." So he said to him, "What is your name?" And he said, "Jacob." And he said, "Your name shall no

longer be Jacob, but Israel; for you have striven with God and with men and have prevailed."

Then Jacob asked him and said, "Please tell me your name." But he said, "Why is it that you ask my name?" And he blessed him there.

So Jacob named the place Peniel, for he said, "I have seen God face to face, yet my life has been preserved." Now the sun rose upon him just as he crossed over Penuel, and he was limping on his thigh (Gen. 32:26-31).

God is looking for a holy generation that will set out determinedly to follow in the train of Jesus' stupendous victory, reckoning that He has broken through every barrier, proceeded through every gate and ridden in triumph through the heavens. He has been given authority to rule from Zion, the house of God, as King of the nations. Therefore His people live as those in the procession of the Lord of hosts, refusing to accept the status quo but rather taking the kingdom by force, in tenacious, almost violent, pursuit of the glory of God. Their eyes are not upon conquest but upon the conqueror, not upon their own glory but upon the King of glory. They are seeking to know God face-to-face and to "stand in His holy place" as a holy priesthood bringing spiritual sacrifices before His throne. They want to be among those who will reign with Him forever.

This, I believe, is the worldview God wants to incorporate into His church, and public praise marching models it in many powerful ways.

So far the processions, parades and marches have occupied our attention as mass expressions, but individuals can also carry the spirit of that procession of praise into their personal lives. In fact, the march is really a mass expression of what is happening in the daily lives of individuals. The apostle Paul with his little apostolic team described himself as being always led by Christ in a triumphal procession, a procession that released a perfume or fragrance into society. To those who were being drawn to Christ, it was the fragrance of life. To those who chose the opposite direction, it was the smell of death (see 2 Cor. 2:14-16).

It would help us if we carry that imagery of a procession into our personal lives, our jobs and our daily business, living in such a way that we leave behind us the fragrance of Jesus as we seek to do all that we do in His name and for His glory.

I am told of a lady in our own church who was going about her weekly shopping in a supermarket. As she went around filling her basket she noticed what a pleasant and joyful atmosphere there was in the place, in stark contrast to her normal experience there. It was so remarkable to her that when she was leaving she mentioned to the checkout girl how everyone seemed so happy in the supermarket that morning. The comment she received was, "It wasn't that way until you came in, my dear. You brought it with you." The presence of God had come with her as she went about her shopping and smiled at other shoppers down the aisles.

Several years ago, after many years of valiant struggle, my sister died tragically of cancer. A few weeks before she died, while she was in the hospital and very weak, she told me this little incident. At that stage of her illness she could barely walk and was constantly on a saline drip. This meant that when she wanted to visit the bathroom at the other end of the corridor, she had to walk slowly, supporting herself on the stand which held the drip which was attached to her arm. In this way one particular night she went down the corridor. The next morning another patient, a woman similarly in the final stages of dying with cancer, told her, "I saw you last night going down the corridor, and it was a wonderful sight. It looked like a religious procession. There was some special glow about you."

My sister was a believer and loved to worship the Lord. I believe that her lonely trek down the corridor was attended by the presence of God, perhaps indeed by angels. In the midst of her suffering she brought with her something of the light and fragrance of Jesus which touched this other patient in a special way.

Perhaps in facing the realities of our personal processions we find the antidote to any tendency toward a foolish triumphalism. Yet God's people through God's power must make every effort of word and deed to bring about some of the lasting changes of the kingdom of God.

We need to guard against praise marching's becoming a glib act of spiritual magic, that with a wave of the magic wand of worship, everything comes to an instant transformation.

In their enthusiasm some folks might think that by having a praise procession, busy centers of sin and injustice will close down overnight. Maybe some will, but I am more and more convinced that the message of Exodus 23:30 is more realistic. That verse says, "Little by little I will drive them out before you, until you have increased enough to take possession of the land" (NIV). If we really want to break Satan's power in a town or city, I think it is going to happen little by little as the church grows in holiness, purity, love, power and authority.

A praise march is undergirded by every other sort of prayer effort. One praise marcher reports:

> In our Soho work we've become convinced that praise marches are just one aspect of spiri-

tual warfare and that the key is an intercession life-style. That means a life-style with all-night prayer, early morning prayer, regular prayer and fasting. Then if you do a praise march that springs out of that sort of life-style it will really have significance. Otherwise, I think there's a danger that something will shift in the atmosphere at the time, but you won't be able to take the ground permanently.

I have found that enduring change results from a full-blown exercise of the entire giftedness of the church. There must also be a dedication to pursue the establishment of refreshed church life at the core of it all. Such efforts are, of course, spearheaded and followed by substantial acts of mercy, attempting to bring forth a beautiful measure of the justice of the kingdom of God.

This kind of full effort is happening the world over. I include one example of a group of believers who are trying to put it all together in Toronto, Canada. The story is told from the point of view of Linda Riesberry, one of the participants:

> In 1988 a team of people, members of the Church of St. George the Martyr, began to get a vision for extending the kingdom of God into other neighborhoods of our parish, but particularly into a very ghetto-ized, inner-city, subsidized housing project called Alexandra Park. The church had worked sporadically in this area for years, but there were no church buildings or a really consistently visible presence within the walls of the project. Many secular agencies worked the area. We were all considered outsiders. Now the time had come for a

consistent Christian presence in that area, maybe even a new congregation. How was this to happen?

I had just come back from a conference at Canterbury very excited about the vision for taking praise, prayer and proclamation to the streets. The prophetic message it had for the church, the gospel message it had for the community and the bold and very visual way the possibilities were presented as to how to act out both the prophetic and the evangelical in the world. I caught a vision of this happening in the housing project, Alexandra Park, where I was building a ministry team. I shared the vision.

Some of us first learned and then tried out some of the music, marching around the inside of the parish church. Then we marched around the courtyard of the church where outsiders might be able to hear us. Then we marched around the church on the street (all this relating to the Sunday Eucharist).

For thirty years we had done the stations of the cross around the neighborhood on Good Friday, stopping at other churches within the parish and where there was a need to pray for various groups, problems and services. It was a kind of prayer walk around the geographical parish.

On this walk in 1989, 1990 and 1991 we focused more on areas where we wanted to plant new congregations; where there was a need for spiritual warfare; where there were some very noticeable community needs; and where a prophetic voice needed to be heard both by the church and the community proclaiming justice and the gospel.

Alexandra Park was an important part of this. By the walk of 1991 we were very publicly the church, particularly in Alexandra Park. People came forward for prayer as we walked through this housing estate and other parts of the parish carrying a six-foot-tall cross. We boldly prayed and proclaimed the kingdom and claimed this area for the Lord.

From the fall of 1988 the Alexandra Park team really began to come together, participating in the broader witness, praying together about their mission and the target of their mission. We just walked and talked and were very visible among the people of the project. There was also a weekly Bible study there that prayed and studied the Scriptures, sang and worshipped with a lot of new music. The church continued for two years just being very visible, building relationships and caring for the community.

In January 1990 all religious groups were barred from the community center. Much prayer was offered, and we entered into real spiritual warfare, but we were certain that "the battle belongs to the Lord." A month later the church was again free to use the center and was declared by the residents' association as "one of us" and not an outsider. We were given a room for our use and some storage cupboards. We placed some praise posters and a large wooden cross on the wall. Our posters and the cross are the only decor that hasn't been vandalized in the center. All a major victory for the Lord!

We decided from the beginning that we need not hide who we were and what we were about. We were there to witness to Jesus Christ and proclaim the kingdom. In June 1990 we decided to have a prayer walk around the housing estate. We asked the president of the residents' association to come with us and identify the needs of the community and the spots where drug dealing went on.

About fifteen of us met to pray in the community center first — four people from the leadership team plus some members from the parish church. Then for an hour and a half we walked quietly through the project praying for needs that included poor maintenance of homes by the housing authority, seniors' care and harassment, families, the children, vandalism, delinquent and uncared-for teenagers, inadequate garbage disposal and a variety of issues relating to crime, drug use and prostitution. Street by street we walked quietly, stopping in front of homes where known problems existed, taking authority over the forces of evil and the illegal drug activity in front of "crack houses" and known drug transfer spots.

As we prayed in front of one house a very anxious-looking resident came out and enquired, "What are you doing?" We told him. He disappeared quickly inside. We heard later that the word had been spread through the project that all drug dealers and drug activity ought to go under cover. They didn't know what we were about, but they figured we were dangerous to them and their activities.

Toward the end of the walk the president of the residents' association told me, "A walk isn't enough. We need a march, a praise and prayer march." He demanded that it be held in two weeks and that the community needed the church to pull it together. We consulted the *Make Way* handbook and began some fast work! We had never dreamed in our wildest dreams that the community would call upon us to do this or that it would be so soon.

The date was set for a Saturday morning, three weeks after the prayer walk. Flyers were distributed to every home in the housing estate and posters were put up. We quickly called on musicians (flute, drums, tambourines, guitars). We set up prayer partners to pray immediately. Large banners each to be carried by two people were made (painted), one with the Toronto skyline (the bottom end of our parish) saying "Shine, Jesus, Shine." The other said, "Fill this place with the Father's glory."

Children in the community center summer program made fifty small placards, some anti-drug slogans and some Christian proclamation. This kind of secular community participation was nothing short of miraculous. Some large supermarket chains and a large bakery company donated enough hot dogs and drinks for five hundred people to use in the celebration at the end of the march. Community leaders contacted the media. The stabbing of a community youth and the beating of his mother by a drug-related gang sparked more interest from all the local TV networks, the three newspapers and the local residents.

People talked about five hundred people showing up. I wondered what I had gotten myself into! I was really moving into unknown and unexpected territory. How were twenty Christians going to lead three hundred to five hundred secular people in a praise and prayer march? How would this not get out of control and not become the usual angry, militant, chaotic protest march?

My prayers and those of our prayer teams increased. My dependence on the Lord was the only way through the fear and the next week of preparation. I was plagued with calls from the media. There were threats from drug dealers. I was confronted by one of the drug lords swinging a baseball bat close to my face. Generally, these men never show up in the projects, but they were threatened by the proposed march! Our prayers and proclamation were seen as violence to the drug dealers. On a local radio station they threatened to meet violence with violence before the march and during the march. Major civic officials, including the mayor, said they were coming. The police were sending a special detachment to protect the mayor and control riots. We cried out to the Lord for protection.

The day of the march we knew peace and the excitement of victory before the march started. Three hundred militant, angry and outraged local residents gathered along with several key politicians, including the mayor of Toronto; six TV stations, including the CBC national news; and the three major Toronto newspapers. We handed out a march program, a route map, a song and shout program and a list of the issues we were praying for. Some local residents offered to carry the portable, handheld sound system. We lined up with banners, placards, clowns, dancers and musicians interspersed among them. I challenged the people to go forth in the name of the Lord, praising Him and thus driving far from this place the snares of the enemy, bringing in the kingdom of God and claiming this turf, the housing estate, for Jesus.

We would march around the boundaries of the project and then down through the center with a few diversions to drug-infested areas. Then someone led us in prayer. A peace descended on the militant crowd, but a determination to go forth prevailed. We began with a song. I had asked the musicians to write a community song for this occasion. The Lord gave them a song that was taken from Jeremiah where God promised to restore the city. This community immediately owned this promise as theirs, and it has become their song, particularly the congregation's.

We proceeded on the march using shouts and songs from the *Make Way* handbook and made up some of our own. We prayed for the same things that were prayed for on the walk. Brick walls that hid crime, drug trade and prostitution were marked with an "X" of masking tape. As each "X" was made, the crowd broke into a spontaneous chorus of "Joshua fought the battle of Jericho...and the walls came tumbling down." When we passed the home of the fellow who had been stabbed (just out of the hospital), my husband, the parish priest, and the mayor went in to pray for the man and his mother. Outside I led all the others in silent prayer for almost five minutes. They were with me in that prayer. All these nonchurch people sang our songs, prayed our prayers and shouted our shouts with full participation. What a mighty God we have!

At the end of the march one of the city council members remarked publicly to the residents that she had never experienced protest against injustice, drugs, complaints against the landlord, the housing authority, and so on done in this manner. It was a most unusual way of doing things but most effective and certainly got our point across! That evening the CBC national TV news showed the walls being marked and the victory of Jesus over drug abuse, crime and injustice being proclaimed.

As we cleaned up after the march, the residents' association president told me that they needed a church *now* in Alexandra Park, in the community center, and *I* was to start it soon. Also very soon we needed to have a candle-light prayer walk at the time the drug dealers were out and bring the light into the darkness of Alexandra Park. We needed to walk and pray through the community at midnight.

Two months later on a Friday evening we walked through the project, starting at midnight, carrying candles, singing quiet choruses and praying at drug-dealing spots. As we were singing, "My peace (light, love) I give to you" one of the local participants (not a member of the church) grabbed hold of my arm excitedly and shouted, "Do you see them go. They run before the light. There are hundreds of them. See them go!" I could see nothing, but I believe he saw demons fleeing by the hundreds before the light of Christ.

The following Sunday we began our first weekly worship. Formal Anglican worship was not what was required here. We had to develop a form of non-Eucharistic worship as I am not ordained. It needed to be simple, very participatory, with lots of singing and ways of praying together.

This group is small. However, the weekly worship is central to all the other activities that go on with this new congregation, known as the Alexandra Park Community Church. We have just celebrated our first anniversary as a worshipping congregation.

Within the past year changes have been made directly as a result of the march. Several "crack houses" have been uncovered, resident drug dealers evicted. Some walls have come down and several others have been marked by the housing authority for demolition. Lighting has been improved.

Yet as the summer came, drug activity increased. We have begun to cover all households with prayer, street by street, house by house, in short prayer walks. This is part of the spiritual battle that we wage in this housing estate. As one of the new church members wrote recently for our diocesan newspapers, "Once again the church decided to head back into Alexandra Park and wage spiritual battle aimed at drug dealers."

The residents also requested another march so that we could give thanks for what had happened and clean up the rest that had to be done. Again we had a praise and prayer march through the housing estate. People came out of their homes asking for healing prayer. Where there was harassment of seniors, we all stopped and prayed for peace and protection and praised God with each one. We celebrated victories where drug houses were gone, where prayer had been answered. One elderly Chinese woman who neither spoke nor understood English joined us as we walked by her and participated fully in the spirit of the march. There are no barriers when in unity with the Spirit!

A personal side to the marches developed. We claimed again this place for the Lord. It finished at the center with a barbecue, followed by a service of worship to mark the first anniversary of the church there. There is a long way to go yet, but the church is there, in a very needy world, proclaiming the love of Christ.

To me this story captures the spirit of public praise as ordinary believers courageously took their faith onto the streets and were overwhelmed with the magnitude of what God did through them. A few months prior to writing this book I visited Alexandra Park.

I was able to verify the evidence of change even in the very infrastructure of the housing project. A recent letter confirmed an estimated sixty-five percent reduction in drug-related activity. The war is not over, but a significant battle has been won.

I also see in this continuing story a beautiful example of how prayer walking, praise marching, social concern and church planting can all combine and interact to positive effect. I believe that this will be repeated in many other places. Rank and file believers who walk their neighborhoods in Spirit-inspired prayer will catch similar visions and receive similar challenges. I expect the results will surpass their expectations and often catalyze the establishment of worshipping communities where none previously existed. The church that goes public in praise will plough up hard ground and scatter seeds that can grow into strong oaks of righteousness.

I see churches cooperating across whole cities to prayer walk systematically every neighborhood, every street, crisscrossing them with faith, offering them back to Him for His glory. In some places this will be done even in a single day. Other places may take several days, a year, or perhaps more until a breakthrough occurs. Cities and nations may unite to do this simultaneously as they have begun to do with March for Jesus. In these and many other ways we will put our feet down, with our lives, to declare throughout the world that the earth is the Lord's and all it contains.

FOURTEEN

ALL THE EARTH
SHALL WORSHIP

A few years ago I was part of a small gathering of worship leaders in London. We represented different streams from the black and white churches and had informally gathered to get to know one another and help build bridges between churches whose worship cultures were very different. The highlight for me was when we worshipped together. During this time, a vision formed in my mind.

I saw the earth as if viewed from space, spinning on its axis, its continents, oceans and islands clearly defined. But then hundreds of threads, each a different color, appeared from out of the nations, arcing out, upward and around the earth, converging above it. As they met, they crisscrossed and weaved in and out of each other over the globe until I could see that something was being woven there. With the multicolored threads still connected to their respective geographical starting points, a gigantic banner had been formed. It hung there billowing gently over the whole globe, overshadowing it. I looked to see whether a design had emerged out of the weaving of the threads. To my joy, on the underside, visible from the earth, was the face of Jesus.

I knew immediately that the multicolored threads represented worship rising to the Lord from believers of every nation, people, tribe and language. The different colors represented the unique gifts of worship that flowed from the nations, a beautiful variety of expressions. The love gifts of millions of hearts lent color and distinctiveness by the contexts of vastly differing cultures. This variety was the very thing that made the forming of the picture possible. Had all the threads been monochrome, the banner would have been blank.

Then followed a special word I believe was meant for those gifted by God to lead others in worship. The essence of it was: "You are the needles carrying the threads into the weaving process. As you let the Holy Spirit weave you in and out of one another in relationship, friendship and worship across the world, so the banner will be formed, and Jesus will be revealed."

At the time, the possibility of an actual worship event that could somehow weave together the worship offerings of many nations seemed remote. Yet we stand on the threshold of it. On May 23, 1992, we will have seen Christians uniting from more than thirty nations, spanning North America and Europe, stretching from Vancouver to Moscow, from Iceland to Albania, totalling in the region of 180 separate marches, filling the streets of cities great and small. In some cities, we are seeing as many as 100,000 praising, praying Christians gathering in one place with one supreme motive, to worship Jesus, the King of the nations.

Their processions move joyfully and purposefully through many gates, some actual gates and some spiritual gates. Some are ancient; some are modern. Many are gates of vision and hope, but the people always follow the One to whom every gate has already opened. A way is being cleared for the rank and file of the churches. They are not ashamed to declare publicly their allegiance to Jesus as they fill street after street with the sound of His praise and the atmosphere of His presence.

Obstacles are being removed. The stumbling stones of fear and unbelief are being taken away, proud mountains of human exaltation are being brought low, and humble valleys inhabited by the meek and lowly of heart are being raised up. A level highway is being constructed, a highway of holiness, in readiness for the grand arrival of the King of kings in a startling paradox of meekness and majesty. Above this great convocation flies one majestic banner, drawing all eyes. It is the face of Jesus, the face that magnetizes the millions of hearts into one adoring focus. His face is earnestly being sought by a generation determined to give Him the glory He deserves in the presence of the nations and of the heavenly powers.

When I was in South Africa recently, a church leader who had just coordinated a nationwide day of marching told me of a vision he had received without previous knowledge of our plans for a global day of marching for Jesus. He said:

> God gave me a vision that showed the world turning. As it turned, the lines of longitude were very prominent and the continental locations were vague. The sun was shining on it from the right-hand side. Slowly, the light from the sun filled each longitudinal segment of the earth, one by one. In each illuminated segment, the various countries could be seen clearly. Each country in that segment was

filled with what must have been millions of Christians, marching up and down the countries with banners declaring that Jesus is Lord. The groups of people marching were representative of every people group in each of the countries.

A vision is being pursued with energy and enthusiasm by believers around the world for a twenty-four-hour period in which marches for Jesus will take place in every capital city. The globe would be circled with a proliferation of joyful celebrations in His honor as the earth spins through the time zones and the sun rises and sets upon people of every tribe and tongue and nation. The languages will be gloriously diverse, but the song will be the same. Nationalities, cultures and skin colors will differ, but we will celebrate as one new man in Christ. As we do we are becoming a demonstration that One greater than the nations is among us.

As Christians unite across the continents and islands to march together, the world will have to ask why we are marching and where we are going. We will tell them that we are marching for Jesus, we are marching with Jesus, and we are marching to Jesus. We will become consistent with that remarkable juxtaposition of imagery in the Song of Solomon, where the king describes his beautiful young bride as being "as awesome as an army with banners" (Song 6:4). We are at the same time the bride of Christ in her wedding procession and the army of God marching in His triumph.

To the worldly wise we may only appear to be a crowd of people getting exuberant in their religion. It may even appear that we have merely succeeded in disrupting the traffic for an hour. Without doubt many will regard our innocent love for Jesus as naive, foolish or dangerous. On the other hand, many who hear the new song will "see and fear and put their trust in the Lord" (Ps. 40:3, NIV).

Calling the Nations to Worship

There is a dimension of worship that is strongly present throughout the Bible but seems rarely to be preached or generally known about. The more I ponder it, the more it seems to me that its force is akin to a current carrying us toward the end of the age. This form of worship is a theme which courses through the rich prophetic veins of the Scriptures, especially the psalms. In Psalm 22:27-28 the psalmist writes, "All the ends of the earth will remember and turn to the Lord, and all the families of the nations will worship before Thee. For the kingdom is the Lord's, and He rules over the nations." And in Psalm 86:9-10 the psalmist observes, "All nations you have made will come and worship before you, O Lord; they will bring glory to your name. For you are great and do marvelous deeds; you alone are God" (NIV).

The prophet Malachi foretells global worship: " 'For from the rising of the sun, even to its setting, My name will be great among the nations, and in every place incense is going to be offered to My name, and a grain offering that is pure; for My name will be great among the nations,' says the Lord of hosts" (1:11). Daniel sees in a vision "One like a Son of Man...and to Him was given dominion, glory and a kingdom, that all the peoples, nations, and men of every language might serve Him" (7:13-14). Perhaps most familiar to believers are the astounding scenes of the book of Revelation, where, as the ages reach toward their climax, people from every nation unite in worship.

Finally, the apostle John describes the scene before the throne: "After these things I looked, and behold, a great multitude, which no one could count, from every nation and all tribes and peoples and tongues, standing before the throne and before the Lamb, clothed in white robes, and palm branches were in their hands; and they cry out with a loud voice, saying, 'Salvation to our God who sits on the throne, and to the Lamb' " (Rev. 7:9-10).

The race which forsook its Creator and worshipped gods of its own invention is being redeemed to its original purpose. Also being redeemed is the whole of creation which had been plunged into decay and disorder through mankind's sin. God is calling willing nations to respond to the love of the crucified One and bow in worship. As I have read passages which relate to processions and marches, I have been struck by how often they carry an appeal to the nations to worship God.

The high point of King David's reign was when in joyful procession he brought back the ark of the covenant to Mount Zion. There he established an unprecedented era of extravagant praise and worship. His song of praise at that time recorded in 1 Chronicles 16:8-36 was peppered with references to universal worship: "Make known His deeds among the peoples...His judgments are in all the earth...Sing to the Lord, all the earth...Tell of His glory among the nations, His wonderful deeds among all the peoples." There is even a specific call to the peoples to bring an offering to the Lord, implying participation in worship before the ark, hitherto assumed to be exclusive to the Jew. "Ascribe to the Lord, O families of the peoples, ascribe to the Lord glory and strength. Ascribe to the Lord the glory due His name; bring an offering, and come before Him; worship the Lord in holy array. Tremble before Him, all the earth...Let them say among the nations, 'The Lord reigns' " (1 Chron. 16:28-31).

As the global dimension of public praise happens, a glorious banner is raised for the nations to rally around.

The banner of Jesus flies above a great and diverse crowd that is going somewhere. They are going up to God to worship, arms laden as it were with choice gifts from every nation. As they go they are calling to the families of the peoples to bring their offerings as well, to join the great procession up Mount Zion, the mountain of the Lord, to stand in the presence of God.

The prophet Micah foretells a scene of universal worship, of nations and peoples streaming to worship and to learn about the ways of God:

> And it will come about in the last days that the mountain of the house of the Lord will be established as the chief of the mountains. It will be raised above the hills, and the peoples will stream to it. And many nations will come and say, "Come and let us go up to the mountain of the Lord and to the house of the God of Jacob, that He may teach us about His ways. And that we may walk in His paths." For from Zion will go forth the law, even the word of the Lord from Jerusalem (Micah 4:1-2).

Whether this present phenomenon of public praise marches has a bearing on any particular scheme of understanding the last days, I am not venturing to speculate. I am not trying to imply that what we are seeing now is a specific fulfillment of the Scripture verses quoted. But there will be such a time, or God is not true to His word. It is enough for me to see that these present events are consistent in character with later events.

Whether this is an early prototype or the first stirrings, whether this is a significant gearshift or an alignment of vision toward a more distant fulfillment, the most important thing at the present moment is obedience. Too much time is spent speculating or arguing about the future while the present opportunity slips away. The present moment is a unique one in church history. I do not know of anything else that has such potential to unite the worldwide church in a conscious act of Christ-centered worship, prayer and proclamation, with a view to taking this gospel to the ends of the earth.

Let us be sure of this, worship in the temple of living stones is well underway. Offerings are pouring in day by day as believers worldwide stream into His gates with thanksgiving and into His courts with praise. As the world of "not yet" believers looks on, they see the radiance on our faces, the reflected glory of the One on whom we are all gazing. They hear our joyful praises and pick up the song we are singing. They feel the holy presence of God and long for cleansing. They are touched by His love and long for His embrace. As our procession of worship moves majestically toward the throne, we call to others to come with us, longing to present them as an offering to the Lamb, that He might receive the rich and full reward of His suffering.

HOW TO PLAN A
MARCH FOR JESUS

Getting Started

As you proceed, remember one critical point: This is a march *for* Jesus. There have been many marches to promote many causes. There have been many marches against many injustices. This is a march *for Jesus*. It is an extravagant demonstration of our love for Him and those He loves. Be careful that nothing distracts from the primary purpose of simply exalting Jesus.

Here is a general overview of how to initiate a March for Jesus in your city.

1. Consult with leaders in your city.

    Involve leaders in planning so they can take ownership of the project. You will encounter strong resistance if you expect leaders to involve their people in an event without consulting with them before you plan it.

2. Register your march with the national headquarters.

    Registering your march will connect you with the expertise of the national and international movement of March for Jesus. A resource package will explain in detail how to organize your own march. You may obtain a registration form by writing to:

March for Jesus U.S.A.
Box 3216
Austin, Texas 78764

3. Dedicate a phone line.

    Designate a phone line that will be answered
    "March for Jesus."

4. Select an organizational committee.

    An organizational committee representing a broad
    spectrum of denominations and churches will dem-
    onstrate unity and avoid the problem of the
    march's being tagged as one church's event. Be es-
    pecially careful that your march lifts up only the
    name of Jesus. Don't allow any *one* church or
    group to place its identity on it. Do not use the
    march to promote any agenda other than simply ex-
    alting Jesus.

5. Choose a route.

    Apply early for proper permits and check on fees.
    See appendix C for ideas about different kinds of
    routes. See appendix D for helpful tips on setting
    up sound systems.

6. Set a budget and raise support.

    Use the budget worksheet from the national head-
    quarters to calculate a budget for your march. Ex-
    penses of the march should be divided between
    participating churches according to their ability.

7. Formalize the commitment of participating churches.

    Start a list of churches which have agreed to partici-
    pate, and add to your list as churches join in the
    planning. Participating churches should be encour-

aged to provide volunteers and financial support.

8. Delegate tasks.

You can delegate tasks to organization committee members or appoint task group leaders who would receive oversight from organizational committee members.

These preliminary steps will help to ensure a successful march. Appendix B contains a planning schedule that will keep your planning on track, starting at five months before the march. Remember, the national headquarters will also provide you with other resource material.

Standing Together

March for Jesus is a coordinated effort not only to take the church to the streets but to do it together. Communication and cooperation will help us stand together in a unified proclamation of love for Christ.

March for Jesus encourages public praise events throughout the year. At the same time, the organization coordinates a special day each year for simultaneous marches on a national and global scale. June 12 has been set as the date for 1993. Those planning praise marches are encouraged to plan an event for that day. The date for the first global march is set for June 25, 1994, to coincide with the Global Conference on World Evangelization in Seoul, Korea.

When you plan a march, please don't neglect to register with the national office. The national office and organization exist so that marches are not just isolated events but one March for Jesus held in various locations. The national office links marches nationally and internationally, gets leaders involved on a national level and publicizes the march on a national level.

Each registered march will be identified by an official name and logo identifying that march with the March for Jesus U.S.A. The name and logo may only be used by permission.

The national office also offers "aids to the vision" to help the marches to be identified together. By producing these aids at the national level, they can provide the consistency and quality needed. Available are: T-shirts, balloons, information handbooks, programs or templates to print your own, posters, radio promotion spots, songbooks, music tapes and press releases.

Getting People Involved

Those who have plannned marches have learned some very helpful tips about getting pastors and people involved. For example:

1. Groups feel better about participating if they are represented in leadership.

2. Do not plan events and expect leaders to participate in them without consulting with them first. Leaders are appreciative when you respect them and ask for their input.

3. Leaders will not get involved if the march puts another demand on their time. Let them give overall approval and delegate someone to represent them. Get the work done through the grass roots.

4. Tasks must be delegated to as many people as possible so that as many people as possible feel responsible for the event. Two things help release people to be productive — a title and a job description. Give as many people jobs as possible.

5. Constantly affirm diversity. This tells diverse groups that their uniqueness is needed. We are not looking for uniformity.

6. Don't give away the vision; give away the implementation. A small group of leaders who understand the vision and have a relationship with one another can give oversight behind the scenes. A diverse group of organizers can take responsibility for implementation.

7. Some pastors will respond if their people express an interest. If the people will lead, the leaders will follow. Have an approach to involve pastors but also a plan to involve people.

A Word of Caution

As we get caught up in the excitement of planning a march, we must guard against allowing anything to steal our focus from Jesus. Here are some things that are desirable benefits of the march but should not be allowed to become the focus.

1. Unity. If we work at unity to the point we become focused on unity, we will get involved in endless relational struggles. If we gather at the cross in humility, we will suddenly find ourselves in unity with each other.

2. Evangelism. The march is not primarily an evangelistic event. Rather it creates a *climate* for evangelism.

3. Spiritual warfare. It's not a down-with-the-devil march. It's simply "up with Jesus." God takes our praise, and Satan suffers terribly.

4. Honorable men. There are many men who are worthy of honor and should be honored but not at the March for Jesus. On that day all recognition, honor and thanks go to Him. Don't introduce anyone but Him.

5. Good causes. At the march a large crowd of people will have gathered. Many will see this as a wonderful opportunity to accomplish something more than just exalting Jesus and prayer. Waste the opportunity, and spend the event totally on Jesus!!

APPENDIX B

PLANNING
SCHEDULE

As you use this schedule, keep in mind that you will depend on three key groups. The leaders of those groups need certain characteristics:

The steering committee focuses on relational unity and should be led by a man of peace.

The organizational committee focuses on functional cooperation and should be led by a man of action.

The task group leaders must accomplish key goals and should be led by a man of action.

The following outline shows what needs to be done to plan a march starting with five months before the date of the event.

Five Months Before the March

1. Pastors' meeting

    a. Discuss strategy to involve other pastors.
    b. Choose a steering committee.
    c. Set a date for the next pastors' meeting.
    d. Make suggestions for organizational committee members.

2. Recruit a volunteer coordinator.

3. Begin a list of participating churches.

4. Apply for a parade permit.

Four Months Before the March

1. Organizational committee meeting

   a. Assign task groups for each member to oversee.
   b. Ask each member to recruit leaders for the task groups they will oversee.
   c. Set the next organizational committee meeting date.
   d. Set the task group leader meeting date.

2. Sign up participating churches.

3. Get lists of volunteers from participating churches.

4. Order T-shirts, tapes and books.

5. Schedule important meeting dates and locations.

Three Months Before the March

1. Task group leader meeting

   a. Introduce each task group leader and his or her task.
   b. Allow time for an exchange of names and contacts of core individuals for each task group.
   c. Introduce the volunteer coordinator.
   d. Distribute a schedule of meetings and key events for task group leaders.

2. Step 1 of training the volunteers

   a. Rally for an overview of the vision and the tasks.
   b. Have a meeting of the task groups.
   c. Solicit offerings, commitments and prayer.

3. Print programs.

4. Begin sales for T-shirts, books and tapes.

5. Get contracts for sound and equipment rental.

Two Months Before the March

1. Step 2 of training the volunteers

    a. Help churches who recently decided to participate to get involved.
    b. Have the task groups meet to prepare further and finalize plans.
    c. Get more prayer!!

2. Send a letter to pastors with an update on progress.

3. Begin rehearsals in churches.

4. Recruit vans and drivers.

5. Distribute publicity material and radio spots.

One Month Before the March

1. Have a final prayer meeting with the pastors.

2. Meet with task group leaders.

3. Continue rehearsals in churches.

4. Begin sales of programs early.

5. Distribute press releases.

6. Ask pastors to make announcements from their pulpits.

CHOOSING A ROUTE

Here is a synopsis of the different types of routes and some of their characteristics and advantages.

1. Direct route

   Participants gather at the starting location (a parking lot or closed street). The march proceeds through an eight- to ten-block part of town to an ending location. A stage and sound system are erected and ready at the ending location. Sound trucks for the march are used to gather the people at the beginning location. Parking is available anywhere in the area between the starting and ending location.

2. Circle route

   The march begins and ends at the same location. Participants gather; the march proceeds around several blocks and returns to the starting location.

3. Multiple routes

   Two or more marches begin at several locations and converge on a central location. This spreads out the parking locations for some of the larger marches.

4. A route unique to your city

Choose a march location with:

a. Historical significance. Redeem past injustices of your city.
b. Prophetic significance. Claim ground or make a statement according to God's direction.
c. Visible targets for prayer. Choose a route that passes by important buildings or locations such as a government building, business district or poverty area. This helps to focus your prayers.
d. Visual impact — Choose a street you can fill with people or use only one side of the street. Close the whole street only if you can fill it. A small march on a major street can look very small and scattered.

APPENDIX D

Sound Amplification

Here are some factors to consider in planning for the sound amplification needs of your event.

1. Sound dissipation. Outside sound dissipates quickly so the dynamics are very different from indoors. You will need to consider:

    a. Singing. Outdoor singing is different from indoor singing because you don't get the encouragement of the echo of other voices. We recommend the use of a recorded program of songs that includes voices. This encourages the participants and helps project what is being sung. Marchers should also be kept in tight formation so they can hear one another. A "live" band on a vehicle also works well, provided that preparation is good. The main disadvantages are 1) shortage of enough bands to cover the number of marching groups, 2) loss of synchronization between bands, and 3) an increase in technical requirements.

    b. Public address system. One sound system will cover a group of approximately two hundred people. Outdoor sound dissipates quickly so you will need a lot more power than the indoor setting. For a small march the sound should not only be adequate volume but even louder to encourage participation of people who are perhaps intimidated by the new, unfamiliar setting.

Important: The speakers must be elevated, or the front of the group gets blasted, and the sound will not travel to the rest of the group. We suggest using vans or pickups and tying the speakers to the top of the vehicle. (The tailgate or bed of the pickup does *not* work well. If trucks are used, speakers should be tied to the top of the cab.)

2. Sound equipment. Most cities have music stores with a sound equipment rental department. This equipment is usually more reliable and portable than church sound systems. One sound system requires:

   a. Two speakers
   b. One amplifier mixer
   c. Two speaker cords
   d. One microphone (optional)

   We suggest one sound system for each two hundred participants, but coverage will vary according to the quality, power and positioning. Never "cut corners" on P.A. provisions because so much depends upon its reliability and effectiveness.

3. Other equipment.

   a. Gas electrical generator. These are available at rental stores. You will need one for each vehicle. If the generator is in the back of a van, leave the doors open to allow ventilation so the driver is not overcome by the fumes. Another option is to run a tube from the generator exhaust out a door or window.
   b. Portable stereos. These allow you to operate by

radio or tape and run them on batteries or an electrical plug. Sometimes plugging them into a generator causes them to pick up electrical noise so having the battery option is good.

c. Wires and connectors. You will need a wire and adapters to go from the headphone jack on a portable stereo to an input on the amplifier.

d. Radio link. If you can arrange for your local Christian radio station to broadcast the march, the radios connected to the sound systems would receive the signal. Your entire march could then be synchronized. The radio station would simply play the tape at the time you designate.

e. Band in a box. Another option would be to play a cassette at each sound source. The groups would not be synchronized, but by separating the groups by about one hundred feet, participants can sing with their group while the next group sings another song at a distance. This creates a parade atmosphere where you hear the next band coming as you hear the one closest to you. It also works well.

f. Noise permit. Many cities require a noise permit any time amplified sound is used outdoors. Check with your parks and recreation department or city government.

g. Sound check. Run a test of one of your sound units several months prior to your event. Even if you have to rent the equipment and the generator, don't skip this step. Check to see if your radio will pick up radio noise from the generator. Your radio will be affected differently on AM or FM. Drive the route to be sure the signal is clear through the entire area.

NOTES

Chapter 5

1. Information about the Salvation Army was derived from the Salvation Army Headquarters Library and its computer archives.

2. Angus Kinnear, *Monsoon Daybreak* (London: n.p., 1971), pp. 64, 109.

3. Angus Kinnear, *Against the Tide*, (Fort Washington, Pa.: Christian Literature Crusade, 1979).

4. From article by James Reapsome, *The Latin American Evangelist*, 1962.

Chapter 6

1. Billy Graham, *Angels: God s Secret Agents* (Irving, Tex.: Word, Inc., 1987), p. 63.

Chapter 8

1. Roger Forster and Paul Marston, *God's Strategy in Human History* (Minneapolis, Minn.: Bethany House).

Chapter 12

1. Winkie Pratney, *Revival: Principles to Change the World* (Springdale, Penn.: Whitaker House, 1983).

Chapter 13

1. Graham Kendrick, "God Put a Fighter in Me," copyright © Thankyou Music.

March for Jesus Resources

1992 MFJ Tee-shirt

Hosanna Integrity's Public Praise Album

Graham Kendrick's Book about Marching for Jesus

Graham Kendrick's Make Way Series available individually or as a set!

March for Jesus
Resource Order Form

Please fill in the form below or photocopy and then send it with payment to:
March for Jesus • 12308 Twin Creek Rd. • Manchaca, Texas • 78652

DESCRIPTION	QTY	PRICE	TOTAL
How to Organize A March for Jesus Packet		$25.00	
Global March Video		$10.00	
"Public Praise" (Graham Kendrick's Book)		$8.00	
MFJ T-shirt (circle size: S M L XL) (XXL +$1)		$10/11 XXL	
March for Jesus Cap		$10.00	
Crown Him (Cassette)		$10.00	
Crown Him (Songbook)		$6.00	
Make Way for Christmas (Cassette)		$10.00	
Make Way for the King of Kings (Cassette)		$10.00	
Make Way for the Cross (Cassette)		$10.00	
Make Way: Shine, Jesus, Shine (Cassette)		$10.00	
4-pack of Make Way cassettes (see list above)		$35.00	
1993 March for Jesus (Cassette) available 9/92		$10.00	
1993 March for Jesus (CD) available 9/92		$14.00	
Please allow 4 to 6 weeks for delivery.		Subtotal	
Please add 10% for shipping & packaging (min. $3.00)			
Texas residents add 6.25% for sales tax			
Total			

Name_____

Address_____

_____ Zip_____

Please check method of payment:
- ☐ Check or money order enclosed (payable to March for Jesus).
- ☐ Charge to my credit card
  - ☐ VISA ☐ Mastercard ☐ Carte Blanche ☐ Discover ☐ Diners Club

Card number_____ Expiration Date_____

Issuing Bank_____ Name on Card_____

Signature_____ Phone (   )_____